D1321354

ARSENAL
On This Day

ARSENAL
On This Day

*History, Facts & Figures
from Every Day of the Year*

PAUL DONNELLEY

ARSENAL
On This Day

History, Facts & Figures from Every Day of the Year

All statistics, facts and figures are correct as of 1st August 2009

© Paul Donnelley
Paul Donnelley has asserted his rights in accordance with the Copyright, Designs and Patents Act 1988 to be identified as the author of this work.

Published By:
Pitch Publishing (Brighton) Ltd
A2 Yeoman Gate
Yeoman Way
Durrington
BN13 3QZ

Email: info@pitchpublishing.co.uk
Web: www.pitchpublishing.co.uk

First published 2009

A catalogue record for this book is available from the British Library.

10-digit ISBN: 1-9054113-6-7
13-digit ISBN: 978-1-9054113-6-8

Printed and bound in Malta by Gutenberg Press

For Bertie Mee MBE, Arsène Wenger OBE
and the Double-winning teams of
1971, 1998 and 2002… and for the team
that will, no doubt, do it again in the future

INTRODUCTION

This is the first Arsenal date book that features only facts, figures and anecdotes directly related to the greatest club in north London. The official book authorised by the club is a lazy effort marred by dozens of facts totally unrelated to Arsenal – which Gooner would care when Port Vale made two trips to Wembley? Or when Chris Waddle left Marseilles to join Sheffield Wednesday? Or when Paul Gascoigne (who?) joined Spurs (who??)? Or when… well, you get the picture.

No, this book features hundreds of Arsenal-centric anniversaries. There are some dates of birth and death but mostly it features events in the 120-plus years of Arsenal's history, which began on 11 December 1886 on a muddy pitch on the Isle of Dogs in east London when… no, you can read it for yourself. Look up your birthday and see which Arsenal-related events happened on that day.

In the introduction to my last book on Arsenal I wrote, "Although Arsenal have not won a trophy for three years now under Mr Wenger, we have a team that is more than capable of winning more silverware for the Highbury House boardroom." Well, another season has gone by without a trophy but Arsenal fans are an optimistic bunch – and with this book you can always relive all the many past triumphs.

Up the Gunners!

Paul Donnelley, 2009
www.pauldonnelley.com

ARSENAL
On This Day

JANUARY

MONDAY 1 JANUARY 1968

Striker Davor Šuker born in Osijek, Croatia. Despite the promise of great things when Arsène Wenger signed him from Real Madrid in 1999, he played just 22 times for Arsenal although he scored eight goals. He failed to set Highbury alight and moved to West Ham United. Šuker had further failed to endear himself to the Highbury faithful by missing a penalty against Galatasaray in the Uefa Cup Final.

FRIDAY 1 JANUARY 1988

Tony Adams became Arsenal's captain, a job he would hold for the next 14 years. It was just before he became club captain that Adams began drinking in earnest. Adams was a fighter for the club on the pitch and increasingly became a brawler in nightclubs.

THURSDAY 1 JANUARY 2009

Former Major League Soccer deputy commissioner Ivan Gazidis began as chief executive replacing Keith Edelman who was sacked in May 2008.

SATURDAY 2 JANUARY 1965

John Radford became Arsenal's youngest ever hat-trick scorer, against Wolves, at the age of 17 years and 315 days, a record that lasts to this day.

FRIDAY 2 JANUARY 1970

Arsenal signed Peter Marinello for £100,000 – the first six-figure transfer fee paid by the club. Great things were expected of the young Scot and he singularly failed to deliver making just one full appearance during the Double-winning season.

SATURDAY 2 JANUARY 1982

Stewart Robson became Arsenal's youngest player in the FA Cup when he played against Spurs. He was 17 years and 55 days old. Arsenal lost 1-0.

SATURDAY 2 JANUARY 1993

Ian Wright scored his fourth hat-trick for the club as Arsenal beat Yeovil Town 3-1 in the FA Cup third round at Huish Park.

TUESDAY 2 JANUARY 2007

Right-back Justin Hoyte scored his only goal for Arsenal, in a 4-0 win over Charlton Athletic. He played 67 times for the Gunners in all competitions.

SATURDAY 3 JANUARY 1998

Arsenal drew 0-0 at Highbury in the FA Cup third round against Port Vale. A replay eleven days later ended 1-1 before Arsenal eventually triumphed 4-3 on penalties.

SUNDAY 3 JANUARY 1999

In *The Sunday Times* Manchester United gaffer Sir Alex Ferguson criticised Arsenal's disciplinary record claiming, "I'll tell you what they do and I've spoken to other managers about this, and they all agree. When Arsenal are not doing well in a game, they turn it into a battle to try to make the opposition lose concentration. The number of fights involving Arsenal is more than Wimbledon in their heyday." He later claimed that he had written to Arsène Wenger to apologise saying he had been "stitched up" – i.e. it was said off the record. Wenger said that "if he sent [an apology], it must have been by horse".

SATURDAY 4 JANUARY 1992

Arsenal again fell victim to FA Cup giant-killers when they lost 2-1 at Wrexham in the FA Cup Third Round.

SATURDAY 5 JANUARY 1907

Woolwich Arsenal lost 5-3 away at Ayresome Park against Middlesbrough and Steve Bloomer scored four goals.

SATURDAY 5 JANUARY 1980

Winger Terry Anderson drowned, aged 35, during a training run in Yarmouth. He had joined Arsenal as a 15-year-old junior in July 1959, becoming an apprentice in August 1960 and signing professional terms a year later in August 1961. He won two England Youth caps but found it difficult to break into the Arsenal side on a regular basis because of George Armstrong, Johnny MacLeod and Alan Skirton. He left for Norwich City in February 1965 for £15,000.

SATURDAY 6 JANUARY 1934

Herbert Chapman, the moderniser of Arsenal, died unexpectedly of pneumonia at his home, 6 Haslemere Avenue, Hendon, Middlesex. He did not live to see Arsenal win the championship for the third consecutive season but he became the first manager of two sides to win the First Division title three years in succession.

WEDNESDAY 6 JANUARY 1971

Arsenal made easy work of non-league Yeovil Town in the FA Cup Third Round. The Gunners beat The Glovers 3-0 at Huish Park in the first match of their successful 1971 campaign.

THURSDAY 7 JANUARY 1988

Striker Charlie Nicholas sold to Aberdeen for £400,000. In his four and a half years at Highbury, Nicholas scored 54 goals in 184 matches but was more infamous for his activities off the field visiting nightclubs and squiring beauties like sexy gymnast Suzanne Dando.

SATURDAY 8 JANUARY 1887

The first match under the name Royal Arsenal played against Erith at Plumstead Common. The Royals won 6-1.

SATURDAY 8 JANUARY 1949

Arsenal beat Spurs 3-0 at Highbury in the FA Cup Third Round, the first time the clubs had met in the competition. Arsenal's goals came from Ian McPherson, Don Roper and Doug Lishman.

FRIDAY 9 JANUARY 1863

Club founder David Danskin born at 11.30pm in Back Street (now Somerville Street), Burntisland, Fife and raised in Kirkcaldy.

SATURDAY 9 JANUARY 1932

Cliff Bastin scored four goals and David Jack hit a hat-trick as Arsenal beat Darwen 11-1 at Highbury in the FA Cup Third Round.

MONDAY 9 JANUARY 2006

Arsenal travelled to Anfield for the quarter-final of the League Cup against Liverpool. It turned into a rout – Jérémie Aliadière, Júlio Baptista (four), and Alex Song Billong all scored as Arsenal won 6-3. It was the first time in nearly 80 years that Liverpool had conceded six goals at home and Arsenal's first League Cup win at Anfield.

SATURDAY 10 JANUARY 1920

Jock Rutherford, Fred Groves, Alex Graham and Fred Pagnam scored in a 4-2 FA Cup first round win over Rochdale at Highbury.

SATURDAY 10 JANUARY 1948

Arsenal were on top of the First Division when Bradford Park Avenue came to visit in the FA Cup Third Round. The visitors became giant-killers as Billy Elliot scored the only goal of the game.

SATURDAY 10 JANUARY 1953

Doug Lishman, Cliff Holton, Jimmy Logie and Don Roper scored as Arsenal beat Doncaster Rovers 4-0 in the FA Cup Third Round.

WEDNESDAY 10 JANUARY 1996

David Ginola sent off as Ian Wright's double gave Arsenal a League Cup fifth round win against Newcastle United at Highbury.

SATURDAY 10 JANUARY 2004

Robert Pires and Freddie Ljungberg scored in the second half as the Gunners beat Middlesbrough 4-1.

THURSDAY 11 JANUARY 1979

Midfielder Brian Talbot signed for Arsenal from Ipswich Town, eight months after he had played for the Tractor Boys in the FA Cup Final victory over the Gunners. In six and a half years at Highbury, Talbot played 327 times for Arsenal and scored 49 times.

SATURDAY 11 JANUARY 1997

Dutch international Dennis Bergkamp was shown the red card and Tony Adams scored in his own net as Sunderland beat Arsenal 1-0.

SATURDAY 12 JANUARY 1952

Arsenal won 5-0 at Norwich City in the FA Cup Third Round. Arsenal would go on to reach the final where they met Newcastle United.

FRIDAY 13 JANUARY 1995

George Graham paid Luton Town £2,000,000 to acquire the services of Welsh-born striker John Hartson, a British record fee for a teenage player at the time. Along with Chris Kiwomya, Hartson was one of Graham's last signings before his sacking the following month. Hartson played 70 times (15 as substitute) for Arsenal, scoring 17 goals before Arsène Wenger sold him to West Ham United. In later years, Hartson became as well known for advertising Advanced Hair Studio, a hair replacement system – which may not have worked as well as he might have liked as today he is totally bald.

FRIDAY 13 JANUARY 2006

Midfielder Abou Diaby signed for the Gunners from Auxerre for around £2million. On the same day Emmanuel Adebayor joined Arsenal from Monaco for an undisclosed fee reported to be £17million.

SATURDAY 14 JANUARY 1933

Arsenal travelled to Fellows Park to play Walsall who were on poor form in the Third Division North. Herbert Chapman rested several first team players while others were unavailable because of a flu epidemic. The Walsall team cost just £69 to assemble, compared to Arsenal, who had spent £30,000 on their superstars. The Saddlers won 2-0 in front of a crowd of 11,150. Interviewed afterwards, Chapman was magnanimous telling the players, "Never mind boys, these things do happen."

SATURDAY 14 JANUARY 2006

Arsenal equalled their biggest win in the Premier League by beating Middlesbrough 7-0 at Highbury. Thierry Henry scored a hat-trick (see 11 May 2005).

MONDAY 14 JANUARY 2008

Arsenal TV launched. Among the first programmes on air was *Arsenal Question Time* hosted by urbane Des Lynam with Arsène Wenger.

SATURDAY 15 JANUARY 1887

Having won their first match 6-0 and their second 6-1, Royal Arsenal beat Alexandria United 11-0.

THURSDAY 15 JANUARY 1891

"One of the Derby chaps was heard to mutter: 'A journey to the molten interior of the earth's core would be rather more pleasant and comfortable an experience than our forthcoming visit to the Royal Arsenal'" – *Derby Post*.

SATURDAY 15 JANUARY 1921

The first derby match after Arsenal's 1913 move to north London played at White Hart Lane in the First Division. Spurs won 2-1.

FRIDAY 15 JANUARY 1999

Arsene Wenger bought 6ft 5½in Nigerian international striker Nwankwo Foluwashola Kanu to Highbury from Italian side Inter Milan for just over £4million. Kanu became a popular figure at Highbury especially after the departure of the Great Sulk. Fans chanted, "Chim chiminy, chim chiminy, chim-chim chiroo, who needs Anelka when we've got Kanu?" After leaving Arsenal for West Bromwich Albion on a free transfer, he signed for Portsmouth where a lot of ex-Arsenal personnel seem to end up. Kanu is the only current Premier League player to have won the Champions League, Uefa Cup, Premier League, FA Cup and an Olympic Gold Medal.

TUESDAY 16 JANUARY 2001

Arsenal eventually signed midfielder Edu from Brazilian side Corinthians for £6million. Arsène Wenger had tried to sign Eduardo César Daude Gaspar in 2000 but the transfer was called off when it was discovered that Edu had a fake Portuguese passport. When his documentation was finally sorted out, he played 79 league games for Arsenal and even contemplated playing for England having gained a British passport but those plans came to nought when he was picked to play for Brazil. On 30 May 2005 he signed for Valencia.

SATURDAY 17 JANUARY 1948

The highest attendance figure for a league match occurred when 83,260 squeezed into Maine Road to watch Manchester United draw 1-1 with Arsenal. Old Trafford had suffered German damage during the Second World War so the Red Devils paid their bitter rivals £5,000 a season plus a share of the gate to share Maine Road.

TUESDAY 18 JANUARY 1977

Supermac Malcolm Macdonald scored a hat-trick at St Andrew's against Birmingham City. Unfortunately, Trevor Francis also scored three for the Blues as the match ended all square.

19 JANUARY 1878

Arsenal's first legendary manager Herbert Chapman born at 17 Kiveton Wales, Kiveton Park, a small mining village in West Yorkshire.

19 JANUARY 1889

Royal Arsenal lost 2-0 to Clapton at their Spotted Dog Ground in Leyton in the semi-final of the London Senior Cup. It was during the match that David Danskin sustained the injury that ended his career.

FRIDAY 20 JANUARY 2006

Theo Walcott aged just 16 signed for Arsenal from Southampton. Before he had made his first team debut, Sven-Göran Eriksson selected him for the England World Cup squad in 2006 although Walcott did not end up playing a game.

SATURDAY 21 JANUARY 1956

Derek Tapscott scored twice at Fratton Park but Arsenal still lost 5-2 to Portsmouth in the First Division.

SATURDAY 21 JANUARY 2006

Midfielder Abou Diaby made his debut in a 1-0 defeat by Everton.

SATURDAY 22 JANUARY 1927

The match at Highbury between Arsenal and Sheffield United became the first to be broadcast live on the radio. Captain H.B.T. Wakelam who wrote three books on rugby (and a week earlier gave the first commentary on a rugger international when his only instruction was "Don't swear") provided the commentary on the match for the BBC, which ended in a one-all draw. As football on the wireless grew in popularity the *Radio Times* published a diagram of the pitch to which the commentator would refer to help listeners know where the ball was. The goal area was known as square one and when players kicked the ball back to the keeper it was back to square one which is where the phrase originates.

TUESDAY 22 JANUARY 2008

Thanks to Arsène Wenger's decision to give young players experience in the first team, Arsenal lost 5-1 to Spurs at White Hart Lane in the second semi-final of the League Cup, the first defeat against the old enemy since November 1999 – eight years and 76 days – and the largest losing margin for 25 years. By half time, 35,979 fans had seen Spurs go two to the good thanks to Jermaine Jenas on three minutes and an own goal from Nicklas Bendtner 24 minutes later. In the second half, Spurs were 4-0 up before substitute Emmanuel Adebayor pulled one back in the 70th minute but Steed Malbranque scored a fifth goal in injury time to put Spurs through to the League Cup Final 6-2 on aggregate. It was the first time that the Gunners had lost after Emmanuel Adebayor scored and the first time Spurs had beaten an Arsène Wenger Arsenal side.

SATURDAY 23 JANUARY 1971

Arsenal stumbled on their way to Wembley and the first Double. The Gunners made hard work of what most commentators assumed would be an easy tie at Fratton Park in the FA Cup fourth round only managing a 1-1 draw with Portsmouth. They did not make it easy for themselves in the 1 February replay at Highbury either only winning 3-2.

SUNDAY 23 JANUARY 2005

Right-winger Jermaine Pennant crashed his Mercedes into a lamppost in Aylesbury while driving drunk, uninsured and serving a 16-month driving ban. When police arrived to arrest him, Pennant told them he was Ashley Cole. Pennant's alcohol reading was 85 micrograms per 100ml of breath. The legal limit is 35 micrograms. On 1 March, he was sentenced to 90 days in prison but released on parole after 30 days on condition he wore an electronic tag at all times – even on the pitch. In April 2005, Pennant signed for Birmingham.

SATURDAY 24 JANUARY 1959

Vic Groves prevented Arsenal being on the end of another FA Cup giant-killing when he scored two goals against Colchester United in a 2-2 draw in the fourth round. Arsenal won the replay comfortably 4-0.

SATURDAY 25 JANUARY 2003

Having seen off Harrogate Town 5-1, Southport 3-0 and Darlington 3-2, non-leaguers Farnborough Town's FA Cup dreams came to an end before 35,108 fans at Cherrywood Road as Arsenal beat them 5-1 with goals from Sol Campbell, Francis Jeffers (2), Dennis Bergkamp and Lauren.

SATURDAY 26 JANUARY 1895

Woolwich Arsenal played Burton Wanderers in a match beset with crowd trouble and unsportsmanlike behaviour towards the referee. As a punishment, the Football League ordered that the Manor Ground be closed for five weeks.

SATURDAY 26 JANUARY 1985

Hoping for a long run, Don Howe saw Arsenal lose 1-0 to York City in the FA Cup fourth round thanks to a penalty from Keith Houchen.

SATURDAY 27 JANUARY 1934

Arsenal walloped Crystal Palace 7-0 at Highbury in the FA Cup Fourth Round. Jimmy Dunne, Cliff Bastin and Pat Beasley each scored twice. Oddly, five of the day's ties saw more than six goals scored by one side.

SATURDAY 28 JANUARY 1899

Derby County inflicted Arsenal's worst defeat in the FA Cup when they smashed six without reply past Roger Ord in the first round tie at Manor Ground, Plumstead.

WEDNESDAY 28 JANUARY 1931

Arsenal beat Grimsby Town 9-1 at Highbury – their greatest win in the First Division – thanks to four goals from David Jack and a Jack Lambert hat-trick. Only 15,751 turned up at Highbury to watch the goalfest. The match was the second attempt, the first match having been abandoned after 63 minutes on 6 December 1930.

DENNIS BERGKAMP AND FRANCIS JEFFERS WERE BOTH ON TARGET IN THE FA CUP ON 25 JANUARY 2003

FRIDAY 29 JANUARY 1988

George Graham bought right-back Lee Dixon from Stoke City for £350,000. Along with David Seaman, Nigel Winterburn, Tony Adams, Steve Bould and Martin Keown Dixon was part of Arsenal's best ever defence – a back four that would give fantastic service under Graham, Stewart Houston, Bruce Rioch and last until the reign of Arsène Wenger. Dixon retired aged 38 in 2002 after helping the club to its third Double.

WEDNESDAY 29 JANUARY 1992

Ray Parlour made his debut at Anfield against Liverpool. Arsenal lost 2-0 and the Romford Pele conceded a penalty.

SATURDAY 30 JANUARY 1937

Arsenal beat Manchester United 5-0 at Highbury in the FA Cup Fourth Round, the highest winning margin over the Red Devils.

WEDNESDAY 31 JANUARY 2007

Having drawn 2-2 at White Hart Lane a week earlier, Arsenal managed to beat Spurs 3-1 after extra time at the Emirates to reach the final of the League Cup for the fifth time. Júlio Baptista had scored both goals at White Hart Lane but today the goals came from Emmanuel Adebayor and Jérémie Aliadière plus an own goal from Spurs defender Pascal Chimbonda.

ARSENAL
On This Day

FEBRUARY

SATURDAY 1 FEBRUARY 1896

Goalkeeper Albert Russell made his only appearance for the club – in the first round of the FA Cup against Burnley and let in six.

SATURDAY 1 FEBRUARY 1958

The last match played in England by the Busby Babes before their ill-fated journey to Belgrade. The result was Arsenal 4 Manchester United 5 and was watched by 63,578 spectators. Arsenal's goals came from Davy Herd, Jimmy Bloomfield (2) and Derek Tapscott scored what would be his last goal for the Gunners before his transfer to Cardiff City. He later commented, "I were the last fella to score against the Busby Babes in England. But I wish to God I wasn't."

WEDNESDAY 1 FEBRUARY 1995

Arsenal met AC Milan at Highbury before a crowd of 38,044 in the first leg of the 1994 European Super Cup – the contest between the winners of the European Cup (now European Champions League) and the European Cup Winners' Cup. AC Milan, managed by future England boss Fabio Capello, had won the European Cup convincingly beating Barcelona 4-0 on 18 May 1994 at the Athens Olympic Stadium in Greece. The previous year they had lost the Super Cup to Parma who had, of course, beaten Arsenal. (Interestingly, Arsenal lost consecutive European finals to teams managed by future England managers.) The Italian side came to Highbury determined to avenge their defeat and to not let the Gunners play. They succeeded returning to Milan having achieved a 0-0 draw.

WEDNESDAY 1 FEBRUARY 2006

Thierry Henry overtook Cliff Bastin's tally of 150 league goals when he scored in the 3-2 home defeat by West Ham United.

WEDNESDAY 2 FEBRUARY 1927

Herbert Chapman sacked first team trainer George Hardy after he began shouting out tactics to the players during a 1-0 home victory against Port Vale in the FA Cup fourth round replay. Chapman put Hardy in charge of the reserves and immediately after the game told the team that Tom Whittaker would not only be the new trainer but also in charge of the team. Oddly, Hardy and Whittaker lived together.

SATURDAY 2 FEBRUARY 1991

Arsenal lost 2-1 to Chelsea at Stamford Bridge, the only league defeat of the 1990-91 season.

WEDNESDAY 3 FEBRUARY 1937

A goalfest between Derby County and Arsenal at the Baseball Ground ended with the Rams winning by the odd goal in nine.

SATURDAY 3 FEBRUARY 1973

Peter Marinello made his last appearance in an Arsenal shirt when he came on as a substitute in the FA Cup against Bradford City. After just 43 first-team appearances, Marinello was off-loaded to Portsmouth.

TUESDAY 3 FEBRUARY 2009

Andrey Arshavin signed for Arsenal at 4.50pm – 24 hours after the transfer window closed thanks to a mix-up with paperwork that needed lawyers to sort out. The striker – given the squad number 23 – cost the club £16.9million from Zenit St Petersburg. Arshavin was so keen to join the Gunners that he hired a private jet to take him from Russia to London on 1 February.

THURSDAY 4 FEBRUARY 1993

Having sold him seven years earlier to Aston Villa for £125,000, George Graham swallowed his pride and paid £2.2million to re-sign Martin Keown. He made 283 league appearances for Arsenal vying for the central defender's position with Steve Bould and Tony Adams. Keown remained at Arsenal until Tuesday 20 July 2004, before being released on a free transfer. He joined Leicester City. He played more than 450 games for the Arsenal and his dedication to the club could never be questioned. During one match, he is said to have yelled at a teammate, "Play like you want to play for the Arsenal."

TUESDAY 4 FEBRUARY 1997

Leeds United under the management of George Graham returned to Highbury where they knocked Arsenal out of the FA Cup by a solitary goal.

SATURDAY 4 FEBRUARY 2006

Emmanuel Adebayor scored on his Arsenal debut in the 2-0 Premier League win over Birmingham City at St Andrew's.

SATURDAY 5 FEBRUARY 1887

Royal Arsenal lost their first-ever match going down 4-0 away to Millwall Rovers.

THURSDAY 5 FEBRUARY 1931

Jack Lambert hit a hat-trick and Cliff Bastin hit a brace as Arsenal beat Leicester City 7-2 at Filbert Street.

TUESDAY 6 FEBRUARY 1894

Full back Ly Burrows made his debut for Woolwich Arsenal against Rotherham Town in a 1-1 draw, almost two years after he signed for the club as an amateur. Eight months later, he signed for Spurs. He played more than 60 times for Arsenal's deadly rivals before returning to Arsenal in October 1895 where he played just one game against Notts County before returning to Tottenham Marshes for two years. He joined Sheffield United in December 1897 but by March 1898 was back at Northumberland Park, Spurs' then home ground after leaving Tottenham Marshes.

WEDNESDAY 6 FEBRUARY 1924

Manager Sir Billy Wright born at Ironbridge, Shropshire. He was appointed manager in 1962 and after an initial good start was unable to bring silverware to Highbury. He was sacked in 1966.

SATURDAY 6 FEBRUARY 1926

The fastest winger in English football Joe Hulme made his Arsenal debut away to Leeds United – the Gunners lost 4-2.

TUESDAY 6 FEBRUARY 1968

Arsenal reached the League Cup Final for the first time by beating Huddersfield Town 3-1 in the second leg of the semi-final, having won 3-2 at Highbury.

SATURDAY 7 FEBRUARY 1903

Woolwich Arsenal lost 3-1 to FA Cup holders Sheffield United in the first round of the competition but 24,000 turned up to watch the match resulting in gate money of more than £1,000 the first time the four-figure mark was reached at Plumstead.

SUNDAY 7 FEBRUARY 1988

Arsenal beat Everton 1-0 at Goodison Park thanks to a Perry Groves goal in the first semi-final of the League Cup and maintained their record of winning every match (as opposed to drawing).

FRIDAY 8 FEBRUARY 1980

Loyal but unlucky goalkeeper Rhys Wilmot turned professional three years after signing schoolboy forms for the club.

WEDNESDAY 8 FEBRUARY 1995

Arsenal met AC Milan at the San Siro for the second leg of the European Super Cup – the contest between the winners of the European Cup and the European Cup Winners' Cup. With no away goals conceded George Graham's men were confident that they could snatch one in Milan. Zvonimir Boban had other ideas and on 41 minutes, he put AC Milan into the lead. With 67 minutes on the clock Daniele Massaro who had scored twice against Barcelona popped up to score Milan's second and clinch them their third Super Cup in six years.

THURSDAY 9 FEBRUARY 1984

Arsenal manager Don Howe signed Ipswich Town forward Paul Mariner for £150,000, a month before his 31st birthday. Mariner scored 14 league goals in 52 games before moving to Portsmouth.

FRIDAY 9 FEBRUARY 2007

Arsenal signed a deal with Major League Soccer club Colorado Rapids, owned by American billionaire Stan Kroenke. The deal was intended to raise Arsenal's profile in America. Managing director Keith Edelman commented, "This is a very important step for Arsenal as this becomes our first venture into the US marketplace." The deal also saw the launch of the Arsenal Cup, a competition open to clubs all over the United States.

WEDNESDAY 10 FEBRUARY 1993

Just 18,253 turned up to Highbury to see Arsenal play Wimbledon – the lowest attendance in the Premier League.

SATURDAY 11 FEBRUARY 1888

Royal Arsenal played their first match at Manor Ground, then known as Manor Field – a 3-3 draw against Millwall Rovers. The pitch was nearly always muddy and to the south behind the goal was an open sewer. Club secretary Elijah Watkins commented that play often had to be stopped while "mud" was wiped off the ball. There were no stands and the club borrowed wagons from the Army for spectators to sit in.

SATURDAY 11 FEBRUARY 1905

Centre forward Andy Ducat made his debut in a 2-0 win against Blackburn Rovers. He lost his place in the following season and switched to play at right half where he became a regular. During his time at Arsenal, he won three caps for England and also won a cap for England at cricket. After 188 matches and 21 goals for Arsenal, he signed for Aston Villa in 1912 for £1,000.

SATURDAY 13 FEBRUARY 1973

Liam "Chippy" Brady turned professional on his 17th birthday.

SATURDAY 13 FEBRUARY 1988

Defender Lee Dixon made his Arsenal debut in a 2-1 home victory over Luton Town. For the next 14 years, he was a regular in the number two shirt making 619 appearances for the club and scored 28 goals.

SATURDAY 13 FEBRUARY 1999

Arsenal met Sheffield United in the FA Cup fifth round at Highbury. Patrick Vieira scored to put Arsenal one-up but Marcelo pulled one back for the Blades. In the 76th minute as United attacked, the ball was cleared but Lee Morris of United was stricken with cramp in the Arsenal box. The ball went to United goalie Alan Kelly who kicked it out of touch so that his teammate could get treatment. Morris went off and Bobby Ford came on as substitute. Ray Parlour took the throw-in for Arsenal and as with the convention threw it in the direction of the Sheffield United goal. Kanu in his first appearance for Arsenal was unaware of the tradition and trapped the ball before crossing to Marc Overmars who scored. Referee Peter Jones awarded the goal. United players were understandably furious and their manager Steve Bruce threatened to get them to leave the pitch in protest. It was six minutes before the game could be restarted. At the final whistle, vice-chairman David Dein and Arsène Wenger discussed the matter and decided to offer to replay the game. The FA agreed to Arsenal's suggestion but Fifa were reluctant fearing it could set a precedent. Finally, they agreed but insisted that both clubs sign a legally binding document stating that they agreed to abide by the result of the rearranged fixture and that part of the gate money must be donated to charity. The game was replayed and Arsenal won 2-1.

TUESDAY 14 FEBRUARY 1989

Arsenal beat France 2-0 in a friendly at Highbury thanks to strikes from Martin Hayes and Alan Smith.

MONDAY 14 FEBRUARY 2005

Arsenal beat Crystal Palace 5-1 at Highbury. The Gunners team did not include one Englishman in the starting line-up. Arsène Wenger said, "When you work on the training ground every day, you don't notice where they're from. I don't even know where I'm from."

SATURDAY 15 FEBRUARY 1992

Sheffield Wednesday came to Highbury and went away crushed as Arsenal won 7-1.

SATURDAY 15 FEBRUARY 2003

Arsenal beat Manchester United 2-0 at Old Trafford in the fifth round of the FA Cup. It was the after match activities that received as much coverage as the game itself. Alex Ferguson was so furious at his team's performance that he kicked a boot across the dressing room that hit David Beckham in the eye necessitating, according to some reports, stitches. Ferguson attempted to play down the incident. "It was a freakish incident. If I tried it 100 or a million times it couldn't happen again. If I could I would have carried on playing!"

THURSDAY 15 FEBRUARY 2007

The Queen held a reception at Buckingham Palace for Arsenal's directors, management and first team squad – the first time a football team has been so honoured leading to a belief that Her Majesty is a Gooner.

SATURDAY 16 FEBRUARY 1991

After his release from prison Tony Adams played his first game for Arsenal in the reserves against Reading at Highbury. The match was scheduled to be played at Elm Park but that ground had a frozen pitch so the game was changed to Highbury where 7,000 or so turned out to cheer Adams in a 2-2 draw.

SATURDAY 17 FEBRUARY 1906

Goalkeeper Jimmy Ashcroft became Arsenal's first England international when he played in the Home Championships against Ireland.

SATURDAY 17 FEBRUARY 1940

The Arsenal Stadium Mystery released. The film was set against the background of a match between Arsenal and The Trojans (played by Brentford in a special kit for the occasion). One of the opposition players drops dead during the match and it is revealed that he has been murdered. But whodunit? His teammates? His ex-girlfriend? Detective Inspector Slade (Leslie Banks) arrives to solve the case. Gunners manager George Allison has a speaking part including the immortal line "One-nil to the Arsenal and that's how we like it" and the rest of the team appear.

WEDNESDAY 17 FEBRUARY 1999

Kanu made his Arsenal debut in the Premier League at Old Trafford against Manchester United in a match that ended nil-all.

WEDNESDAY 18 FEBRUARY 1987

Tony Adams made his England debut against Spain in Madrid as England triumphed 4-2.

SATURDAY 19 FEBRUARY 1916

Retired full back Bob Benson made a rare visit to Highbury to watch his former club play Reading. As the crowd waited for the match to begin, a murmur went up that the Arsenal were a man short – Benson's former full-back colleague Joe Shaw was unable to get permission from the munitions factory to play. Benson stepped into the breach and pulled on an Arsenal shirt for the 54th time. It was the first time he had played in more than a year and his lack of match fitness showed. During the second half, he collapsed with exhaustion on the pitch. He staggered to the bench but was still unable to catch his breath. Trainer George Hardy helped him to the dressing room but despite his ministrations Benson died in the trainer's arms, aged just 33. He was buried in his Arsenal shirt.

SATURDAY 20 FEBRUARY 1937

In the FA Cup fifth round Ted Drake hit four at Turf Moor as Arsenal beat Burnley 7-1.

SATURDAY 20 FEBRUARY 1999

Nicolas Anelka scored a first half hat-trick against Leicester City but looked so miserable for the entire second half that he earned the nickname the Incredible Sulk.

TUESDAY 21 FEBRUARY 1995

Former Manchester United full back Stewart Houston took over as caretaker manager for the first time following the sacking of George Graham for his involvement in "financial irregularities". Graham called Arsenal's decision "a kangaroo-court judgment".

TUESDAY 21 FEBRUARY 2006

Arsenal became the first English team to beat Real Madrid at the Santiago Bernabeu winning 1-0 thanks to a strike by Thierry Henry.

SATURDAY 21 FEBRUARY 2009

Andrey Arshavin made his debut for Arsenal in the disappointing 0-0 Premier League draw at the Emirates against Sunderland. Carlos Alberto Vela replaced Arshavin after 63 minutes.

TUESDAY 22 FEBRUARY 1949

Striker John Radford born at Hemsworth, Yorkshire. He spent twelve years at Highbury making 379 appearances and hitting the back of the net 111 times.

THURSDAY 23 FEBRUARY 1989

After 12 years at Highbury during which time he understudied Pat Jennings, George Wood and John Lukic, goalie Rhys Wilmot signed for Plymouth Argyle for a fee of £100,000 after playing 340 representative games for Arsenal.

SUNDAY 23 FEBRUARY 1997

Arsène Wenger spent £500,000 to bring a young French forward from Paris Saint-Germain. Nicolas Anelka would go on to become one of Wenger's best signings but fell from favour with the fans, a situation not helped by his apparent lack of enthusiasm for being at Highbury.

SATURDAY 24 FEBRUARY 1951

A former crane driver in Wales, Jack Kelsey made his debut for Arsenal against Charlton Athletic at Arsenal Stadium – and let in five goals.

WEDNESDAY 24 FEBRUARY 1988

Having beaten the Merseysiders at their home ground Arsenal comfortably beat Everton 3-1 in the second leg of the League Cup semi-final. Michael Thomas, David Rocastle and Alan Smith provided the goals that took Arsenal back to Wembley to defend their trophy.

SATURDAY 25 FEBRUARY 1933

Arsenal walloped Blackburn Rovers 8-0 at Highbury in the First Division.

SUNDAY 25 FEBRUARY 2007

Arsenal played Chelsea in their fifth League Cup Final and the first all-London affair. The match was played at the Millennium Stadium, Cardiff. The two teams had met at Cardiff in the 2002 FA Cup Final so Chelsea were looking for revenge. Arsenal kicked off the incident-packed game and after 11 minutes, Theo Walcott scored his first goal for Arsenal. Eight minutes later, Didier Drogba scored the equaliser for Chelsea – his 27th goal of the season. On 28 minutes, Denílson became the first player to be booked and eight minutes later he was joined in referee Howard Webb's notebook by Chelsea's Michael Essien for a late tackle on Júlio Baptista. By the end of the match, Webb had issued seven yellow cards and three reds. On the 84th minute Drogba headed Chelsea into the lead. Thanks to an injury to John Terry, seven minutes of stoppage time were added. In the 96th minute, an altercation resulted in red cards for Arsenal's Kolo Touré and Chelsea's Mikel John Obi and then substitute Adebayor also received a red card for getting involved. Wenger said, "It suddenly exploded. It was strange, as it didn't reflect the quality of the game. Suddenly we lost it and they lost it as well and it became a brawl. I'm not sure the referee picked the right ones out but he made a decision. I believe we were unlucky with some decisions from the referee. Their first goal was offside." The full-time whistle eventually blew in the 103rd minute of play.

SATURDAY 26 FEBRUARY 1966

Forward Joe Baker joined Nottingham Forest for £65,000, having scored a ton of goals for Arsenal.

SATURDAY 26 FEBRUARY 1983

Pat Jennings became the first player to appear in 1,000 first class matches when he kept goal against West Bromwich Albion at the Hawthorns – and Big Pat kept a clean sheet in the goalless draw.

SATURDAY 27 FEBRUARY 1932

Thanks to a Herbie Roberts goal Arsenal beat Huddersfield Town 1-0 at Leeds Road in the sixth round of the FA Cup. The match attracted the largest ever crowd – officially 67,037 – to Huddersfield's ground but an estimated 5,000 more broke in and hundreds watched the game from the side of the pitch. The *Huddersfield Examiner* reported that many fans fainted, two were crushed and a hundred or so more had to be treated for injuries in the club's gym.

SATURDAY 28 FEBRUARY 1981

Utility player Steve Walford made his last appearance in an Arsenal shirt during a 2–2 draw against Middlesbrough. In March 1981, he moved to Norwich City for £175,000 (Willie Young would also play for Arsenal, Spurs and Norwich.)

SUNDAY 28 FEBRUARY 1993

Tony Adams and some friends went to Towcester racecourse. Afterwards they went to a nightclub where Adams fell down a flight of concrete stairs necessitating 29 stitches in a head wound. A week later, Arsenal beat Ipswich Town 4-2 at Portman Road in the FA Cup Quarter Final and Adams won the man of the match title.

MONDAY 29 FEBRUARY 1904

Inside-left Tom Shanks hit a hat-trick as Woolwich Arsenal beat Burnley 4-0.

ARSENAL
On This Day

MARCH

SUNDAY 1 MARCH 1987

Full-back Viv Anderson and striker Niall Quinn scored a goal each to beat Spurs 2-1 in the League Cup semi-final at White Hart Lane and force a replay.

SATURDAY 2 MARCH 1968

Arsenal played Leeds United before 97,887 spectators in their first League Cup Final. The match ended 1-0 to the Yorkshire side. Bobby Gould said, "Jack Charlton used to volley you up in the air and Norman Hunter used to thwack you on the way down." In the second half, all 22 players became embroiled in a brawl after Charlton fouled Jim Furnell in the Arsenal goal.

THURSDAY 2 MARCH 2000

Arsenal beat Deportivo la Coruña 5-1 in the first leg of the Uefa Cup fourth round to record their first victory over a Spanish team.

SATURDAY 3 MARCH 1906

At Plumstead Woolwich Arsenal beat Birmingham City 5-0 to equal their biggest winning margin against the Blues from the Midlands.

SATURDAY 3 MARCH 2007

The biggest attendance at the Emirates (so far): 60,132 against Reading in a 2-1 victory for Arsenal.

SATURDAY 4 MARCH 1933

Arsenal first wore red shirts with white sleeves in a match against Liverpool. The Gunners lost 1-0.

WEDNESDAY 4 MARCH 1987

After two League Cup semi-final matches ended 2-2 on aggregate, this third game was played at White Hart Lane before 41,005 fans, three days after Arsenal had beaten Spurs 2-1 again at White Hart Lane. For that tie away goals did not count double so the two teams were forced to meet again to settle the contest. For the third successive time ex-Gunner Clive Allen put Spurs ahead. It looked as if Spurs were on their way to Wem-ber-ley and things were not helped when Charlie Nicholas was carried off injured. However, the chaps from White Hart Lane did not anticipate Arsenal's never say die attitude and with just eight minutes to go substitute Ian Allinson levelled the scores. At 9.44pm in injury time David "Rocky" Rocastle popped up to slide the ball under Ray Clemence in the Spurs goal and break Tottenham hearts.

TUESDAY 4 MARCH 2008

Arsenal became the first English team to beat AC Milan at the San Siro, winning 2-0.

SATURDAY 5 MARCH 1994

Ian Wright scored his fifth hat-trick for Arsenal as the Gunners beat Ipswich Town 5-1 at Portman Road.

SATURDAY 5 MARCH 1977

Red-headed centre-half Willie Young made his debut against Ipswich Town at Highbury. The Tractor Boys ran out 4-1 winners. Terry Neill commented, "He tried to play like Pele, George Best and Gerson rolled into one. He should have remembered that he was a 14-stone Scotsman."

WEDNESDAY 6 MARCH 1935

Tottenham Hotspur 0 Arsenal 6 – Arsenal's biggest away win over Spurs – was not so much a match as a massacre and it was only the woodwork and the Spurs goalie that stopped the goals for Arsenal being in double figures.

THURSDAY 6 MARCH 2008

The development that was Highbury topped out. The plan is to turn the stadium into Highbury Square, a series of 711 small and costly apartments with the pitch area becoming a communal garden. The East and West Stands have been preserved in the new development, which is expected to open in 2010. Chief executive Keith Edelman, clad in a hard hat and fluorescent jacket over his suit (despite the toastmaster standing next to him clad normally) gave a speech.

SATURDAY 7 MARCH 1891

Royal Arsenal won yet another trophy after beating St Bartholomew's Hospital 6-0 in the London Senior Cup Final.

WEDNESDAY 7 MARCH 2007

Thierry Henry played his last game for Arsenal – a 1-1 home draw with PSV Eindhoven in the European Champions League.

SATURDAY 8 MARCH 1958

Goals from David Herd (three), Danny Clapton and Jimmy Bloomfield gave Arsenal the edge in a nine-goal thriller against Chelsea at Highbury.

SATURDAY 9 MARCH 1935

Highbury saw its biggest ever attendance: 73,295 turned up to watch a First Division match against Sunderland. The match ended 0-0.

THURSDAY 10 MARCH 1898

Woolwich Arsenal's first professional manager Thomas Mitchell resigned after just seven months in the chair, as the team sat in fifth place in the Second Division. On his watch, Arsenal played 26 games, winning 14, a 53 per cent success rate.

SATURDAY 11 MARCH 1972

Brendon Batson became the first black player to represent Arsenal when he came on as a substitute against Newcastle United at St James' Park. Arsenal lost 2-0.

WEDNESDAY 11 MARCH 1981

Terry Neill signed Welsh midfielder Peter Nicholas from Crystal Palace for £400,000. Nicholas played just 57 league games for Arsenal in a disappointing two years at Highbury.

MONDAY 12 MARCH 1900

Arsenal achieved their biggest ever win in the league beating Loughborough Town 12-0 in the Second Division. Despite the glut of goals, only 900 people had turned up to watch.

WEDNESDAY 12 MARCH 1913

Inside forward Jimmy Blair killed himself. He was 27. He made just thirteen first-team appearances for Arsenal and scored three times before being sold to Manchester City for £150 in November 1906.

WEDNESDAY 13 MARCH 1957

Manager, journalist and commentator George Allison died of a heart attack at his Golders Green home ten years after retiring as Arsenal boss.

FRIDAY 14 MARCH 1980

The beautiful Mercedes McNab born at Vancouver, British Columbia, Canada. The only child of Double star Bob McNab, she appeared in *Buffy The Vampire Slayer* as Harmony Kendall after losing the title role to Sarah Michelle Gellar. Voted one of the 25 sexiest Celebrities by *Playboy* in 2007, she posed naked for the magazine in November 2006, and said, "It's funny. My real name sounds like a stripper name, too. But, that's what I was given at birth. I always asked my mum why and she would say, 'Oh, it's because I really liked it.' But I'm convinced it's because they had a Mercedes when I was born and that I was conceived in it." (See 25 March 1973)

SATURDAY 14 MARCH 1998

Arsenal travelled to Old Trafford knowing a win would put them on course to win the title. Arsenal's defence held out capped by a great performance by stand-in goalie Alex Manninger replacing the injured David Seaman. Marc Overmars played brilliantly running rings round the United defence and coming close to scoring on several occasions. On 79 minutes, Anelka played Overmars on and the Dutchman put the ball neatly through Peter Schmeichel's legs for the only goal of the game.

SATURDAY 15 MARCH 1884

Manager Leslie Knighton born at Church Gresley, Derbyshire. He was in charge at Highbury as secretary-manager from 1919 until Sir Henry Norris sacked him during the close season of 1925. Under his rule, Arsenal never finished higher than mid-table, their best performance being ninth in 1920–21.

SATURDAY 15 MARCH 1969

A year on from the defeat by Leeds and Arsenal were back at Wembley in the League Cup Final hoping to win the only domestic trophy that had so far eluded them. Arsenal were expected to win easily against Third Division Swindon Town but not for the first time the minnows upset the form book and after extra time ran out 3-1 winners. Bobby

Gould scored Arsenal's goal. The main consolation was that because Swindon were a Third Division side they were not allowed to take up their prize as participants in the European Fairs Cup so Arsenal who wore gold and blue for the match were given their place.

MONDAY 15 MARCH 1976

Goalie Jack McClelland died of cancer, aged just 35. McClelland was intended to replace Jack Kelsey but he broke a collarbone and soon found he was fighting for the number one jersey with Jim Furnell. McClelland left for Fulham in December 1964.

SATURDAY 15 MARCH 1997

Goalkeeper Lee Harper made his one and only appearance for the first team in a 2-0 win over Southampton in the Premier League.

SATURDAY 16 MARCH 1935

Arsenal travelled to Goodison Park to play Everton in the First Division. The home crowd began to shout at the Arsenal players labelling them "southern poofs" which didn't please Arsenal's Wilf "Iron Man" Copping. Within five minutes of the start of the second half, Copping took out Everton's Jack Coulter who had been amused by the crowd's chanting. Fellow Evertonian Will Creswell was furious and decided to get his revenge. On 70 minutes, he and Copping went for the same ball and Creswell split open the Arsenal man's shinpad. Five minutes later, Copping tackled Creswell and sent the Toffeeman over the hoarding and onto the terrace. Moss and Drake scored as Arsenal won 2-0.

THURSDAY 17 MARCH 1949

Right-back and assistant manager Pat Rice born at Belfast, Northern Ireland but raised in London.

TUESDAY 17 MARCH 2009

Arsenal beat Hull City 2-1 in the FA Cup Quarter-Final at the Emirates after going 1-0 down through Nick Barmby on 12 minutes. Robin Van Persie, captaining Arsenal for the second time, and William Gallas scored the goals that took Arsenal into a semi final – the club's 26th – with Chelsea. It was Arsenal's 27th consecutive unbeaten game in the FA Cup, going back to 1997.

TUESDAY 17 MARCH 2009

Highbury Square, the development that used to be Highbury, awarded a prize for architectural excellence.

WEDNESDAY 18 MARCH 1970

On their way to their first trophy for seventeen years, Arsenal beat Romanian side Dinamo Bacău 7-1 in the fourth round of the European Fairs Cup.

THURSDAY 19 MARCH 1992

Goalkeeping legend Jack Kelsey died aged 62. In thirteen years he appeared between the sticks 356 times for the Gunners. On his retirement from playing, he ran the Arsenal shop.

SATURDAY 20 MARCH 1926

Jock Rutherford became the oldest player to represent Arsenal when he turned out aged 41 years and 159 days old against Manchester City at Highbury in a first division match – and Rutherford used all his experience as he helped Arsenal to a 1-0 win.

FRIDAY 20 MARCH 1998

Having failed to unseat England keeper David Seaman from the number one position at Highbury, Vince Bartram, who had joined the club for £40,000 from Bournemouth on 10 August 1994, signed for Gillingham in a bid to play first-team football. He stayed with the Kent club for almost six years.

SATURDAY 21 MARCH 1896

Caesar Jenkyns became Arsenal's first international player. He played for Wales in their 4-0 defeat by Scotland.

SATURDAY 21 MARCH 1964

John Radford made his first team debut against West Ham United in a 1-1 draw at Upton Park.

SATURDAY 21 MARCH 2009

Goalie Manuel Almunia saved his third penalty of the season as Arsenal beat Newcastle United 3-1 at St James' Park.

SATURDAY 22 MARCH 1890

Royal Arsenal won their first title – beating Thanet Wanderers 3-0 in the final of the Kent Senior Cup held at Chatham.

WEDNESDAY 22 MARCH 1950

Arsenal beat Chelsea 1-0 at White Hart Lane to reach the FA Cup Final. The teams had drawn the first semi, also at the home of Tottenham Hotspur, 2-2 and Freddie Cox scored in both games.

MONDAY 22 MARCH 1976

Double-winning Bertie Mee announced that he would stand down as Arsenal manager at the end of the season.

SATURDAY 22 MARCH 1986

Don Howe resigned as manager and replaced by Steve Burtenshaw. Rumours abounded that the board had approached Terry Venables to be Gunners manager, which had forced Howe's hand.

SATURDAY 23 MARCH 1907

Woolwich Arsenal reached the semi-final of the FA Cup for the second consecutive year. However, as with 1906 they were unable to progress to the final, losing 3-1 to Sheffield Wednesday at St Andrew's despite taking an early lead through a Bill Garbutt header.

WEDNESDAY 23 MARCH 2005

Arsenal chairman, Peter Hill-Wood unveiled an English Heritage Blue Plaque commemorating Herbert Chapman at the manager's home from 1926 until his death eight years later, 6 Haslemere Avenue, Hendon, Middlesex.

THURSDAY 24 MARCH 1994

George Graham sold 29-year-old Swedish winger Anders Limpar to Everton for £1.6million. Limpar scored 20 goals during his time at Highbury.

TUESDAY 24 MARCH 2009

Sixteen Arsenal players appeared on international duty for the 2010 World Cup qualifying matches.

SUNDAY 25 MARCH 1973

Full back Bob McNab appeared as a footballer called Bob in "The Football Match" episode of the hit sitcom *On The Buses*. Stan Butler (Reg Varney) and Jack Harper (Bob Grant) are desperate to win £5 each in a football match and McNab is brought in as a ringer – until Stan crocks him during training but even then the opponents, the Basildon Bashers, are not what the bus crew from the Luxton and District Traction Company expected.

FRIDAY 25 MARCH 1988

Winger Brian Marwood signed for Arsenal from Sheffield Wednesday for a fee of £600,000. Marwood made 52 league appearances in two and a half years at Highbury.

THURSDAY 26 MARCH 1987

One of Arsenal's best if underrated forwards Alan Smith joined the Gunners from Leicester City for £750,000. Manager George Graham immediately loaned Smith back to Filbert Street for the rest of the season. Before his enforced retirement at 32, Smith played in more than 300 games for Arsenal scoring 115 goals.

FRIDAY 26 MARCH 1999

At Knightsbridge Crown Court Graham Rix was sentenced to 12 months in prison for having underage sex with a 15-year-old girl and indecently assaulting her. Rix was believed to have met the girl and had sex with her at a west London hotel on the eve of Chelsea's Premier League match with Manchester United in February 1998. Passing sentence, the judge said, "These offences took place when she was only weeks short of her 16th birthday, the age of consent, yet at the time of the offences she was a virgin, plainly a girl who was undoubtedly like any other fascinated and flattered by the attentions of a man who was to her knowledge a celebrity, attended by the glamour of fame and success. There was in my view a significant amount of irresponsibility in your behaviour, illustrating a determination to have sex irrespective of her feelings." The judge pointed out that Rix had refused to use a condom despite the girl's requests and his knowledge that she was a virgin at the time. He served six months of his sentence and, on release, was placed on the sex offenders' register for 10 years. Chelsea gave him his old job back.

SATURDAY 27 MARCH 1971

Hard man Peter Storey's penalty earned Arsenal a 2-2 draw in the FA Cup semi-final against Stoke City and kept the Gunners' Double Dream alive.

SATURDAY 28 MARCH 1931

Centre-half Herbie Roberts won his only cap for England, playing against the Auld Enemy at Hampden Park. England lost 2-0 and Roberts was never selected again.

GOOD FRIDAY 28 MARCH 1986

Goalie Rhys Wilmot made his first team debut for Arsenal, six years after he turned professional. Arsenal won 4-1 at Villa Park against Aston Villa.

SATURDAY 29 MARCH 1975

Striker Frank Stapleton made his first-team debut in the 1-1 draw against Stoke City.

SATURDAY 30 MARCH 1895

Woolwich Arsenal played Newton Heath for the first time and won 3-2. Newton Heath later changed its name to Manchester United.

MONDAY 30 MARCH 2009

American tycoon Stan Kroenke increased his stake in Arsenal to slightly more than 20 per cent, at a cost of £42.5million. He bought 5,000 ordinary shares at £8,500 apiece from fellow Gunners director Danny Fiszman. He said, "After having been invited to join the board last year I am delighted to be able to increase my shareholding in Arsenal. I will continue to work closely with my board colleagues to maintain the stable environment in which the club operates and to preserve the self-sustaining business model enjoyed by the club."

SATURDAY 31 MARCH 1906

Woolwich Arsenal reached the semi-final of the FA Cup for the first time. Having seen off the challenges of West Ham United, Watford, Sunderland and Manchester United, they were unable to beat Newcastle United, losing 2-0 at the Victoria Ground, Stoke.

SATURDAY 31 MARCH 1973

Bertie Mee controversially substituted Frank McLintock during a 1-0 home defeat by Derby County. It turned out to be McLintock's last game for the Gunners and in June 1973 Mee sold him to Queens Park Rangers for £25,000. Mee preferred to entrust the centre of defence to Jeff Blockley.

SATURDAY 31 MARCH 1979

Arsenal beat Wolverhampton Wanderers 2-0 in the FA Cup Semi-Final at Villa Park. Former Gunner John Barnwell managed Wolves.

SATURDAY 31 MARCH 2001

One of Arsenal's most popular players in the Eighties and Nineties David Rocastle died aged 33 from non-Hodgkin's lymphoma. Later that day, Arsenal played Spurs at Highbury and in Rocastle's memory beat the Lillywhites 2-0, the first goal coming from Robert Pirès wearing Rocky's old number seven shirt.

ARSENAL
On This Day

APRIL

FRIDAY 1 APRIL 1949

Left-back Sammy Nelson born at Belfast and signed for Arsenal on his 17th birthday in 1966. Sammy Nelson originally played on the left wing but Bertie Mee converted him to the left-back position where he understudied Bob McNab.

SATURDAY 2 APRIL 1927

The fastest winger in English football made his England debut against Scotland at Hampden Park. Arsenal's speedy wideman Joe Hulme was one of four debutants that day before 111,214 fans. England won 2-1 and he went on to play nine times for his country and score four goals.

FRIDAY 3 APRIL 1914

Woolwich Arsenal dropped the geographical location from their name. For a time the club was known albeit unofficially as The Arsenal until 1926 when Herbert Chapman insisted the club should drop the definite article.

SATURDAY 3 APRIL 1926

Tom Parker, the first Arsenal captain to hold aloft a trophy, made his debut in a 4-2 home win against Blackburn Rovers. Between today and Thursday 26 December 1929 (a 2-1 home defeat by Portsmouth), he played 172 times for the Gunners – the most consecutive appearances for the club.

TUESDAY 3 APRIL 1979

After scoring an own goal, left-back Sammy Nelson pulled one back for Arsenal against Coventry City at Highbury and then celebrated by flashing his bare backside to the North Bank. Terry Neill suspended his defender.

THURSDAY 3 APRIL 2008

Goalkeeper Manuel Almunia signed a long-term extension to his contract with Arsenal with his aim to complete his playing days at Highbury. The Spanish-born keeper said, "I talked to my wife and I said I did not want to go back to Spain to play. Hopefully I can finish my career here."

SATURDAY 4 APRIL 1914

The first competitive match after Woolwich Arsenal became simply Arsenal saw a 1-1 draw at home to Bristol City. Tom Winship scored.

SUNDAY 4 APRIL 1993

Two years after losing another FA Cup Semi-Final saw Arsenal out for revenge against Spurs. The game looked as it was heading for a 0-0 stalemate when Arsenal won a free kick in the 79th minute. Paul Merson flicked a ball into the Spurs area and Tony Adams popped up with a header to score the only goal of the game. Arsenal's celebrations were somewhat muted by Lee Dixon's sending off but were on their way to becoming the first team ever to win both domestic cups.

FRIDAY 4 APRIL 1997

Fever Pitch, the film based on Nick Hornby's autobiographical work, was released. It starred Colin Firth as English teacher Paul Ashworth and Ruth Gemmell as his girlfriend Sarah Hughes. The film's advertising tagline was: "Life gets complicated when you love one woman and worship eleven men". The final scenes for the film, set around the time of Arsenal's championship-winning match at Anfield, were shot outside Highbury. By the time the film came to be made Highbury's terracing had changed so the footage of fans on the terraces was shot at Fulham's Craven Cottage.

SATURDAY 4 APRIL 2009

Arsenal beat Manchester City 2-0 at the Emirates to take their unbeaten run to 17 games – the longest run of any Premier League team in 2008-09.

EASTER SATURDAY 5 APRIL 1890

Royal Arsenal won their second trophy of the season beating Old Westminsters 3-1 in the final of the London Charity Club at Spotted Dog Ground in Leyton.

SUNDAY 5 APRIL 1987

Finally... Arsenal won the one domestic trophy that had eluded them for so long: the League Cup. A 96,000 Wembley crowd watched as Charlie Nicholas scored both goals as Arsenal beat Liverpool 2-1.

THURSDAY 5 APRIL 2007

ITV sold their 9.99% shareholding to Stan Kroenke's KSE UK Inc. Kroenke was listed 153 in *Forbes*' list of the wealthiest 400 Americans – seven places higher than the Glazer family who own Manchester United and 89 ahead of Aston Villa owner Randy Lerner.

SATURDAY 5 APRIL 2008

Defender Armand Traore made his Premier League debut for Arsenal against Liverpool.

SATURDAY 6 APRIL 1895

A goal glut begun as Woolwich Arsenal beat Crewe Alexandra 7-0 and then put six past Walsall (while conceding one) on 12 April at home in the Second Division. In fact, it was almost a farewell present as Arsenal have not met Crewe in any competition since 1896.

TUESDAY 6 APRIL 1920

Tom Whittaker made his debut in a 1-0 defeat away to West Bromwich Albion. He played 64 Division One games and six FA Cup matches for the Gunners before injury forced his retirement. He became trainer and later manager.

MONDAY 7 APRIL 1952

In a repeat of the match two years earlier Arsenal finally beat Chelsea in the FA Cup semi-final after a replay but this time a rather more convincing 3-0 rather than 1-0. All four matches (semi-final and replay in 1950 and 1952) were played at White Hart Lane. Sadly, in 1952 unlike in 1950, Arsenal did not go on to lift the trophy.

TUESDAY 7 APRIL 2009

Arsenal drew 1-1 with Villarreal at El Madrigal in the first leg of the European Champions League quarter-final. Villarreal continued their unbeaten at home record and it was the first time that Robert Pirès had played against the Gunners.

SATURDAY 8 APRIL 1978

Arsenal beat Orient 3-0 at Stamford Bridge in the FA Cup semi-final. Former Gunner Jimmy Bloomfield was manager of the Os at the time.

TUESDAY 8 APRIL 2008

Liverpool broke Arsenal's heart as they won 4–2 to knock them out of the Champions League 5–3 on aggregate. It was the third meeting for the two teams in six days with both other games ending one-all. Arsenal scored through Abou Diaby and Emmanuel Adebayor but it was not enough to beat the Merseysiders.

WEDNESDAY 8 APRIL 2009

England youth international striker Luke Freeman, 17, signed professional terms with Arsenal. On 10 November 2007 he had made history by playing for Gillingham in an FA Cup tie against Barnet aged 15 years and 233 days – the youngest player to appear in the FA Cup.

EASTER MONDAY 9 APRIL 1917

Half-back Spencer Bassett died in France of wounds received in the First World War. He was 31.

WEDNESDAY 9 APRIL 1980

Arsenal drew 1–1 with Juventus at Highbury in the first leg of the European Cup Winners' Cup semi-final. With the valuable away goal and the fact that no English team had ever won in Turin, the odds favoured the Italians but the experts reckoned without a curly-headed Gunner called Paul Vaessen.

GOOD FRIDAY 9 APRIL 2004

Battling to protect an unbeaten record in the league (the first team since Preston North End in 1888-1889 to go through a whole season unbeaten) and an attempt to win the Premier League, Arsenal faced Liverpool at Highbury. At half-time Liverpool led 2–1 but a hat-trick by Thierry Henry and one from Robert Pirès gave Arsenal a 4–2 victory. Gerard Houllier, the Liverpool manager, said, "They showed why they are unbeaten in the league."

SATURDAY 10 APRIL 1948

Arsenal won their first major post-war trophy capturing the First Division championship with a 1–1 draw with Huddersfield Town at Leeds Road.

SATURDAY 10 APRIL 1954

Arsenal legend Joe Mercer ended his career. As Arsenal beat Liverpool 3-0 at Highbury he broke his leg in two places during a collision with teammate Joe Wade. Mercer, 39, was carried off to a standing ovation from the 33,178 fans.

SATURDAY 11 APRIL 1998

Goalkeeper Alex Manninger conceded a goal against Newcastle United – the first time he had been beaten in nine Premier League matches stretching back to 31 January when he took over from the injured David Seaman. He set a club record of eight clean sheets in consecutive league matches.

SATURDAY 11 APRIL 2009

Alex Song Billong scored his first Premier League goal as Arsenal beat Wigan Athletic 4-1 at JJB Stadium.

TUESDAY 12 APRIL 1994

Having drawn 1-1 at Parc des Princes, Paris in the first leg of the European Cup Winners' Cup semi-final, Arsenal beat Paris St-Germain 1-0 at Highbury to reach the final.

SATURDAY 13 APRIL 1895

Arsenal goalie Harry Storer became the first player to gain representative honours when he played for the Football League against the Scottish League. 1895 was the season that Arsenal wore red and light blue striped shirts including the goalkeeper – it was not until 1909 that the goalie wore a different shirt to the rest of the team.

EASTER MONDAY 13 APRIL 1998

On their way to the Double in Arsène Wenger's first full season in charge Arsenal beat Blackburn Rovers 4-1 at Ewood Park.

SUNDAY 14 APRIL 1991

Tottenham Hotspur and Arsenal met for the first time in the FA Cup Semi-Final with Arsenal attempting a second Double. Troubled genius Paul Gascoigne scored from a free kick 30 yards out after just five minutes to put Spurs ahead. Gary Lineker put the Lillywhites two-up but Alan Smith scored for Arsenal to make it 2-1 at half time with everything to play for. It was not to be Arsenal's game and Lineker added a third to seal the game for Spurs.

SATURDAY 15 APRIL 1972

For the second year in succession Arsenal were drawn against Stoke City in the FA Cup semi-final and for the second year in succession, the match had to be decided by a replay. In the first match at Villa Park Arsenal goalie Bob Wilson was injured and unable to continue despite receiving "encouragement" from teammate Peter Storey (what ITV commentator Brian Moore used to call "giving him stick"). John Radford went in goal while substitute Ray Kennedy moved into Radford's position. Thanks to a goal from George Armstrong, Arsenal managed to hang on for a replay at Goodison Park on 19 April, which they won 2-1 with goals from Charlie George (penalty) and John Radford. Geoff Barnett took over in goal against a Stoke side that included Gordon Banks and ex-Gunner George Eastham.

SATURDAY 16 APRIL 1977

Gay icon Freddie Ljungberg born at Vittsjö, Hässleholm, Sweden. He became as well known for his interesting hairstyles and modelling underwear as for anything he did on the field. Ljungberg joined Arsenal in 1998 for £3million, then the biggest transfer fee for a Swedish player. That same year he was nominated as one of the world's sexiest men.

WEDNESDAY 17 APRIL 1985 ˙

Charlie Nicholas and Brian Talbot scored as Arsenal beat Spurs 2-0.

EASTER MONDAY 18 APRIL 1927

Right-half turned centre-half Herbie Roberts made his debut against Aston Villa four months after Herbert Chapman paid Oswestry Town £200 for his services. Moved from midfield to central defence Roberts became an integral part of the team in the WM formation that Chapman and captain Charlie Buchan if not pioneered then certainly popularised.

SUNDAY 18 APRIL 1993

In 1992-93, Arsenal created history by becoming the first team to win both major domestic cup competitions in the same season. In addition, oddly, their opponents on both occasions were Sheffield Wednesday and on both occasions, the result was 2-1 to the Gunners. The first match, the League Cup Final, was staged at Wembley before 74,007 fans. Arsenal's goals came from Paul Merson and Steve Morrow (his first for the club at senior level) although 22-year-old Morrow was unable to enjoy most of the post-match celebrations. At the final whistle the captain Tony Adams had picked Morrow up and promptly dropped him breaking his arm in the process and necessitating oxygen for the utility player. The match was the first match in which any European clubs had used squad numbers on their shirts instead of the usual one to 11 (see 15 May 1993).

WEDNESDAY 18 APRIL 2007

Arsenal vice-chairman David Dein was sacked after "irreconcilable differences" with the rest of the board. He had joined the board in 1983 and at the time chairman Peter Hill-Wood described Dein's investment as dead money. Dein went on to become one of the most powerful men in British football. On the same day chairman Peter Hill-Wood denied the club was being sold to American billionaire Stan Kroenke. "The shareholders would prefer to stay in control than sell out to some stranger," he said. "We would be horrified to see ownership of the club go across the Atlantic. [Danny Fiszman, Lady Bracewell-Smith and the Carr family have] no intention of selling. These people love Arsenal, they are independently wealthy and do not need the money. Having a few extra million pounds in the bank is of no interest to them. We're here for Arsenal football club, not to make a few bob. The club has been run for the benefit of supporters, staff and players." (See 1 May 2009)

SATURDAY 18 APRIL 2009

Despite an opening goal from Theo Walcott in the 18th minute, Arsenal lost 2-1 to Chelsea at Wembley in the FA Cup Semi-Final – the first time the Blues had beaten Arsenal since 1957 in the FA Cup.

MONDAY 19 APRIL 1915

Manager George Morrell resigned after seven years in the chair.

WEDNESDAY 19 APRIL 1972

Arsenal beat Stoke City 2-1 in the FA Cup semi-final replay played at Goodison Park. Charlie George and John Radford hit the goals that took Arsenal to Wembley for the second consecutive season.

WEDNESDAY 19 APRIL 2006

Kolo Touré scored the last goal under floodlights at Highbury against Villarreal in the first leg of the Champions League semi-final.

FRIDAY 20 APRIL 1973

Former captain Eddie Hapgood suffered a fatal heart attack while attending a sports forum at Honiley Hall, Warwickshire. He was 64.

WEDNESDAY 20 APRIL 1983

Goalkeeper George Wood made his last appearance for Arsenal in the First Division against Norwich City, a game Arsenal lost 3-1. In both his first and last games for the club, he was on the losing side.

THURSDAY 20 APRIL 1995

Having lost the manager two months earlier, few rated Arsenal's chances of silverware under caretaker manager Stewart Houston. However in the European Cup Winners'Cup semi-final at Highbury on 6 April they beat Italian side Unione Calcio Sampdoria 3-2 only to have that score reversed today when they visited Genoa. When extra time failed to separate the two teams, the match was decided on penalties and Arsenal ran out 3-2 winners.

MONDAY 21 APRIL 1930

Arsenal drew 6-6 with Leicester City at Filbert Street, having been 3-1 down – the first 6-6 draw in the Football League.

TUESDAY 21 APRIL 1970

Left-back Sammy Nelson made his international debut for Northern Ireland against England as a sub but at Arsenal he was still playing second fiddle to Bob McNab.

TUESDAY 21 APRIL 2009

Andrey Arshavin scored all four goals as Arsenal drew 4-4 with Liverpool at Anfield before a crowd of 44,424.

WEDNESDAY 22 APRIL 1970

Arsenal played RSC Anderlecht at the Parc Astrid in Belgium before 37,000 fans in the first leg of the European Inter Cities Fairs Cup. The Belgian club won by a comfortable (or so they thought) 3-1 with substitute Ray Kennedy getting one back for the Gunners. Kennedy had only played twice for the first team prior to the game and had made two further appearances as a substitute.

SATURDAY 22 APRIL 1978

Irish full-back John Devine made his debut for the Gunners, in a 3-1 win over Leeds United. It was the first victory at Elland Road in almost forty years and the first game in which Arsenal were captained by goalie Pat Jennings.

TUESDAY 22 APRIL 1980

Paul Vaessen scored against Juventus in the final moments of the European Cup Winners' Cup semi-final to make Arsenal the first British team to win in Turin.

SATURDAY 23 APRIL 1927

Arsenal made their first FA Cup Final appearance at Wembley against Cardiff City before 91,206 fans. Arsenal lost 1-0. It was the first and only time the FA Cup has left England and it was the infamous final when Arsenal goalie Dan Lewis seemed to have a shot from Cardiff's Hughie Ferguson covered only for it to slide into the goal off his shiny new jersey with just 16 minutes remaining. Since then almost every Arsenal goalkeeping jersey has been washed before it is worn.

SATURDAY 23 APRIL 1932

Arsenal's third visit to Wembley for the FA Cup Final was against Newcastle United. Bob John opened the scoring with a header but the Magpies hit the back of the Arsenal net twice, to win 2-1. Arsenal became the first team to score first at Wembley and still lose.

SATURDAY 24 APRIL 1915

Arsenal played their last game in the Second Division against Nottingham Forest and won 7-0 at Highbury. Harry King hit four, Jock Rutherford added another and Bob Benson scored two a year before his untimely death.

WEDNESDAY 24 APRIL 1974

Jimmy Rimmer made his debut between the sticks for Arsenal at Anfield where Arsenal beat Liverpool 1-0. It was his only match of the season but in 1974-75 he played in all but two league games for Arsenal. Seen as a long-term replacement for Bob Wilson, Rimmer only spent three seasons at Highbury and left for Aston Villa when Terry Neill signed Pat Jennings.

SUNDAY 24 APRIL 1988

Arsenal returned to Wembley to defend the League Cup where they met Luton Town. Despite goals from Martin Hayes and Alan Smith, 95,732 spectators watched Luton win 3-2.

MONDAY 25 APRIL 1904

Woolwich Arsenal drew 0-0 with Port Vale in their last home game of the season – the season that saw them promoted to the First Division. Arsenal had won all but their last two games and scored 67 goals at home conceding just five. In home and away matches they scored 91 goals and let in just 22.

MONDAY 25 APRIL 1932

Leslie Compton made his debut against Aston Villa in a 1-1 draw at Villa Park. For a brief period, he was club captain. He retired from playing in July 1953 at the age of 40 and became a coach at Arsenal for three years until May 1956. He played more than 250 games for Arsenal but his wartime record was even more impressive than little brother Denis. In 131 games, he scored 93 goals – a strike rate of 71 per cent. In February 1941, he scored 10 goals in one game against Clapton Orient. Leslie Compton played cricket for Middlesex from 1938 until 1956 where he kept wicket. In 1947, Middlesex won the County Championship, making the Comptons the only brothers ever to have won the national title in both football and cricket.

SATURDAY 25 APRIL 1936

Arsenal returned to Wembley for the third time in the 1930s and this time the opponents were Sheffield United. 93,384 fans saw Ted Drake score the only goal of the game 15 minutes from time as Arsenal won their second FA Cup six years after their first triumph. Remarkably there were no newsreel cameras to capture the events.

SUNDAY 25 APRIL 2004

Rarely is victory sweeter than when it is achieved at the home of a bitter rival. Patrick Vieira and Robert Pirès scored Arsenal's goals in a 2-2 draw at White Hart Lane that brought the Premier League trophy to Highbury.

WEDNESDAY 25 APRIL 2007

Red-headed squeaky voiced midfield dynamo Alan Ball died aged 61 of a heart attack while trying to put out a bonfire at his home in Warsash, Hampshire. He was the second member of the 1966 England World Cup-winning team to die.

SATURDAY 26 APRIL 1913

Woolwich Arsenal played their last match at the Manor Ground, Plumstead, a one-all draw against Middlesbrough watched by just 3,000 people. Once the venue was no longer home to football, the ground became derelict. It was later demolished and the land redeveloped. Today it is an industrial estate once more. The Manor Ground was on the land that is now Nathan Way, Griffin Manor Way and Hadden Road.

SATURDAY 26 APRIL 1930

Arsenal's second cup final and the first time they won the FA Cup in their 44-year history. The Arsenal beat Huddersfield Town 2-0 at Wembley before 92,488 spectators. On 16 minutes, Alex James opened the scoring putting the ball into the bottom corner of Huddersfield goalie Turner's net. With Arsenal one up, the LZ127 Graf Zeppelin flew over the stadium. The engine noise made the fans look up and distracted them from the game. It was the first FA Cup Final in which the captains – Tom Parker and Tom Wilson – led the teams out side by side.

SATURDAY 26 APRIL 2008

At 1.15am Perry Groves arrested in Crouch Street, Colchester for being abusive. A police spokesman said, "Police issued a 43-year-old man from Colchester with a fixed penalty notice for a Section 5 public order offence of using abusive and insulting words and behaviour, likely to cause harassment."

SUNDAY 26 APRIL 2009

Keeper Manuel Almunia set a new club record of eight consecutive clean sheets at home – stretching back to Arsenal's 1-0 win over Portsmouth on 28 December 2008. The record ended when Łukasz Fabiański was between the posts against Chelsea as the Gunners lost 4-1.

SUNDAY 27 APRIL 2003

Thierry Henry voted PFA Player of the Year, an award he would again win the following year. He also won the Football Writers' Association Footballer of the Year award in 2002-03, 2003-04 and 2005-06.

TUESDAY 28 APRIL 1970

Arsenal won their first European trophy and first trophy since Joe Mercer's men in 1953 when they beat RSC Anderlecht 3-0 before 51,612 spectators at Highbury (4-3 on aggregate) in the second leg of the European Inter Cities Fairs Cup.

WEDNESDAY 28 APRIL 1982

Goalie George Wood won his fourth and last international cap for Scotland, playing against Northern Ireland.

MONDAY 29 APRIL 1912

Arsenal beat Spurs 3-0 at White City in a charity match to raise money for survivors and the families of those who died on the *Titanic*.

SATURDAY 29 APRIL 1950

Arsenal won the FA Cup beating Liverpool 2-0 with both goals coming from Reg Lewis, one either side of half time. Incredibly, Arsenal captain Joe Mercer trained with the Liverpool team in the run-up to the final – he had a greengrocer's business in Wallasey. His teammates travelled to Brighton to take the air.

WEDNESDAY 29 APRIL 2009

Manchester United beat Arsenal 1-0 at Old Trafford in the first leg of the European Champions League Semi-Final.

TUESDAY 30 APRIL 1974

Arsenal's long-serving goalie Bob Wilson made his last appearance in the first team in a 1-1 draw at home to Queens Park Rangers. Wilson had played in 41 of the 42 league games in his final season giving way just once to Jimmy Rimmer, the man who had been bought to replace him. The match also marked the last appearance of Ray Kennedy.

FRIDAY 30 APRIL 1993

Former centre-half Tommy Caton died of a heart attack brought on by years of alcoholism that culminated in him drinking two bottles of gin a day. Caton was just 30.

ARSENAL
On This Day

MAY

SATURDAY 1 MAY 1937

Alex James played his last game for the Gunners a "dismal" according to Bernard Joy nil-all draw at home to Bolton Wanderers. Despite his onfield partnership with Cliff Bastin, Bastin said he found his teammate's broad Scottish accent "a trifle incomprehensible".

FRIDAY 1 MAY 1953

Arsenal beat Burnley 3-2 to capture their seventh league championship. The match began with a flurry of attacks for Arsenal but Burnley counterattacked and Roy Stephenson put them into the lead. Arsenal, often dangerous when behind, played some brilliant football and within 11 minutes were 3-1 ahead thanks to goals from Alex Forbes, Doug Lishman and Jimmy Logie. Arsenal seemed to have the game in the bag and relaxed slightly, only for Billy Elliott to pull one back for the Clarets. Burnley pushed forward to get an equaliser but Arsenal pulled everyone back into defence. It was too much for Tom Whittaker who retired to the dressing room, a bag of nerves. He stayed there until the jubilant players returned to tell him that they had won – the game and the league title. The championship was won by a narrow margin – Arsenal's goal average was 1.51 while second place Preston North End's was 1.41.

TUESDAY 1 MAY 1962

After a 3-2 defeat to Everton, on the final game of the season, George Swindin resigned as Arsenal boss to be replaced by Billy Wright.

THURSDAY 1 MAY 2008

Managing director Keith Edelman sacked in a surprise move that shocked football. In his eight years at the club, Edelman was instrumental in the move to the Emirates Stadium, oversaw the redesign of the club badge and saw Arsenal's turnover break the £200million mark.

FRIDAY 1 MAY 2009

Director Stan Kroenke became the largest shareholder at the club, increasing his stake to 28.3 per cent. Kroenke bought 4,839 shares valued at between £8,500 and £10,500 each from members of the Carr family, including director Richard Carr (see 18 April 2007).

SATURDAY 2 MAY 1992

Ian Wright scored a hat-trick as Arsenal beat Southampton 5-1 in the last game before the North Bank was pulled down.

SATURDAY 2 MAY 2009

Arsenal beat Portsmouth 3-0 at Fratton Park – the fifth match in a row away from home that they had scored three or more goals. It equalled a record set in the 1932-33 season. Coincidentally, the fifth game in that season was also against Portsmouth at Fratton Park although that match ended 3-1 to the Gunners. It was also remarkable that none of the seven subs on the Arsenal bench had ever started a Premier League match.

SATURDAY 3 MAY 1952

Arsenal lost 1-0 to Newcastle United in the FA Cup Final before another Wembley full house of 100,000. The Arsenal team was beset with injuries both before and during the game. Ray Daniel played with a broken wrist, Doug Lishman had a septic wound and Jimmy Logie had internal bleeding from a leg wound.

MONDAY 3 MAY 1971

Arsenal beat Spurs 1-0 at White Hart Lane in the last match of the 1970-71 season and won the league championship – the first half of their first Double. The Arsenal team repaired to the White Hart pub in Southgate for a private party where they drank until the early hours.

SATURDAY 3 MAY 1980

Goalie Paul Barron made his last appearance in a green shirt for Arsenal as the Gunners beat Coventry City 1–0.

SUNDAY 3 MAY 1998

Arsenal beat Everton 4-0 at Highbury to win Arsène Wenger's first league title in his first full season in charge. Marc Overmars with two, Tony Adams and an own goal provided the goals.

TUESDAY 4 MAY 1976

The first man to lead Arsenal to the Double, in 1971, Bertie Mee resigned as manager.

MONDAY 4 MAY 1987

Midfielder Cesc Fàbregas born at Vilessoc de Mar, Casal de Curacion, Spain. He joined Arsenal in September 2003 from Barcelona.

WEDNESDAY 4 MAY 1994

Arsenal met Parma (managed by Sven-Göran Eriksson) in the European Cup Winners' Cup Final in Copenhagen's Parken Stadium. Ian Wright was unable to play because a yellow card in the semi-final against Paris St Germain meant that he was suspended while John Jensen was out with an injury. David Hillier and Martin Keown were also missing and David Seaman played with a pain-killing injection in his ribs. Parma, the holders of the trophy, were favourites to retain the trophy. Only 33,765 fans watched Alan Smith score Arsenal's winner on 21 minutes. Once they had the goal, Arsenal's defence put up the shutters as they so often did and Parma in all yellow with blue trim found that they could not break them down.

SATURDAY 4 MAY 2002

Arsenal returned to the Millennium Stadium in Cardiff for their second consecutive FA Cup Final determined to avenge the defeat a year earlier by Liverpool. Ray Parlour scored first on 70 minutes and 10 minutes later Freddie Ljungberg made it 2-0 to the Gunners. Ljungberg, having also scored in the 2001 final, became the first man to score goals in successive FA Cup finals since Bobby Smith of Tottenham Hotspur, who scored in 1961 and 1962. The attendance was 73,963. The victory gave Arsenal their third Double.

SATURDAY 5 MAY 1934

David Jack retired after scoring 139 goals for Arsenal in 234 matches at all levels.

THURSDAY 5 MAY 1966

Only 4,554 turned up to Highbury to watch Arsenal lose 3-0 to Leeds United. It was Arsenal's lowest ever attendance for a first class match.

TUESDAY 5 MAY 2009

Arsenal dumped out of the European Champions League when they lost 3-1 at home to Manchester United (4-1 on aggregate). It made it four seasons without any silverware in the Highbury House boardroom. The match had a number of unfortunate firsts for Arsenal: it was the first time Arsenal had lost a European match at home; it was the first time that they had conceded three goals at home in Europe and it was the first time that Arsenal had lost a European semi-final.

SATURDAY 6 MAY 1916

Arsenal played a Rest of London Combination team in a testimonial (the first of its kind) for Bob Benson's widow after he died at Highbury before a crowd of more than 5,000. His death was later ascribed to a burst blood vessel. The match finished, not that it mattered, in a two-all draw.

SATURDAY 6 MAY 1939

Arsenal beat Brentford 2-0 in the First Division – the last match of the 1938-39 season and Arsenal's last official league fixture before the outbreak of the Second World War. The match was filmed and used in the movie *The Arsenal Stadium Mystery*. Brentford represented The Trojans and played in a special kit for the occasion.

SATURDAY 6 MAY 1972

Hoping to retain the FA Cup that they had won against Liverpool the year before, Arsenal lost to Leeds United at Wembley. During the 70s Arsenal visited Wembley for the FA Cup four times, winning twice and losing twice.

SATURDAY 6 MAY 1978

Arsenal returned to Wembley to meet Ipswich Town in the FA Cup Final. Terry Neill was facing his first of three consecutive FA Cup finals. One hundred thousand people saw Paul Mariner and George Burley almost score for the Tractor Boys but the woodwork and Pat Jennings saved Arsenal. After 76 minutes, Ipswich attacked and Willie Young mis-hit his clearance, the ball landing at the feet of Roger Osborne who belted it past Jennings to take the cup by the now familiar scoreline of 1-0.

SUNDAY 6 MAY 1990

Due to meet his teammates at Highbury to go on tour, Tony Adams had one for the road at a party in Braintree and somehow ended up at a barbecue in Rainham. At 3pm Adams thought it was about time he joined his teammates and jumped into his Ford Sierra to drive to Heathrow. At 80mph Adams lost control and crashed into a front garden demolishing the front wall. When he was breathalysed, Adams was more than four times over the legal drink-drive limit. The police allowed Adams to join the Arsenal team and a friend drove him to Heathrow where he boarded a plane for the 13-hour flight to Singapore.

MONDAY 6 MAY 1991

Arsenal won the title with two games to spare when Nottingham Forest beat Liverpool 2-1. Later on, Arsenal beat Manchester United 3-1 at Highbury in celebration.

SATURDAY 7 MAY 1988

Curly-haired midfielder Graham Rix made his last appearance for Arsenal in the league in a 2–1 win against Everton. In all he played 464 times for the Gunners, scoring 51 goals. On retirement, he joined Chelsea's coaching staff and even played once for them in the Premier League in May 1995 during an injury crisis – ironically against Arsenal.

WEDNESDAY 7 MAY 2003

Right-back Justin Hoyte made his debut for Arsenal in the 6-1 victory over Southampton. In August 2008, after 68 appearances and one goal, he signed for Middlesbrough, thus preventing him playing first-class football for Arsenal with younger brother Gavin and becoming the first brothers to do so since the Comptons.

SUNDAY 7 MAY 2006

Arsenal played their last game at Arsenal Stadium, Highbury, "The Home of Football" – a 4-2 victory over Wigan Athletic with a hat-trick from Thierry Henry.

FRIDAY 8 MAY 1942

Arsenal's youngest captain and manager William John Terence Neill born at Belfast, Northern Ireland. He joined Arsenal in December 1959.

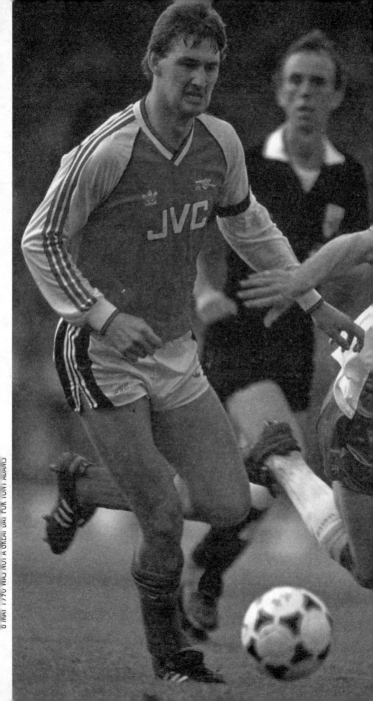

SATURDAY 8 MAY 1971

Arsenal beat Liverpool 2-1 at Wembley to win the FA Cup and complete their first Double. After 90 minutes the scores were level and two minutes into the first period of extra time Steve Heighway broke through Arsenal's defences and put the ball past Bob Wilson. Liverpool had only conceded one goal in the competition up to the final, so Arsenal's Double dreams looked in tatters. Arsenal picked themselves up and Eddie Kelly scored the vital equaliser (George Graham also claimed the credit) after 101 minutes. With nine minutes left on the clock, Charlie George got the ball twenty yards from Ray Clemence's goal and let fly with a shot that gave the goalie no chance.

WEDNESDAY 8 MAY 2002

Arsenal beat Manchester United 1-0 at Old Trafford before 67,580 fans to achieve their third Double. Sylvain Wiltord scored the only goal. Arsenal also became the first team for more than a century to go an entire season unbeaten away from home. Arsène Wenger said, "What this team has achieved is tremendous and will remain in history. This is not only a team of good players, it is one of togetherness." The ever-magnanimous Alex Ferguson said, "They are scrappers who rely on belligerence – we were the better team."

FRIDAY 8 MAY 2009

England starlet Theo Walcott signed a new long-term contract with Arsenal.

SATURDAY 9 MAY 1936

Bernard Joy became the last amateur to play football for England when he represented his country against Belgium.

MONDAY 9 MAY 1966

Arsenal won the FA Youth Cup for the first time beating Sunderland 4-1 in the second leg of the final, having lost the first leg 2-1. Dave Simmons scored in both legs but despite this promising start he never progressed to the first team. In the Arsenal side that day were two young men who did, Pat Rice and Sammy Nelson.

SATURDAY 9 MAY 1987

Full back Viv Anderson played his last game for Arsenal in a 2-1 defeat against Norwich City at Highbury. He played 170 times for Arsenal at all levels.

SUNDAY 10 MAY 1959

Arsenal's secretary-manager Leslie Knighton died aged 75, eleven years after he retired to Bournemouth.

SATURDAY 10 MAY 1980

Arsenal reached the FA Cup Final for the third consecutive year but lost 1-0 to Second Division West Ham United.

WEDNESDAY 10 MAY 1995

Arsenal played Real Zaragoza at the Parc des Princes in Paris defending their European Cup Winners' Cup before 42,424 spectators. With George Graham's sacking, Stewart Houston took charge of the team. John Hartson scored for Arsenal, equalising after Juan Esnáider had put the Spaniards ahead. At 90 minutes, the referee blew for full time and an extra 30 minutes loomed. With penalties looming, on the 120th minute ex-Spurs player Nayim spotted that Seaman was off his line and lobbed him from 40 yards winning the game for Real Zaragoza.

SUNDAY 10 MAY 2009

Arsenal suffered their heaviest league home defeat at the Emirates, losing 4-1 to Chelsea.

MONDAY 11 MAY 1925

Arsenal advertised in *Athletic News* for a team manager, insisting that "Gentlemen whose sole ability to build up a good side depends on the payment of heavy and exhorbitant (sic) transfer fees need not apply".

SATURDAY 11 MAY 2002

After a 4-3 win over Everton at Highbury, before a crowd of 38,254, skipper Tony Adams lifted the Premier League trophy as Arsenal achieved their third Double.

WEDNESDAY 11 MAY 2005

Arsenal played their last game at Highbury in red and white shirts. They beat Everton 7-0 – their biggest win in the Premier League – before playing in redcurrant shirts for the last season at Highbury.

SATURDAY 12 MAY 1979

Arsenal met Manchester United at Wembley in the last FA Cup Final of the 70s. There were 15 internationals on the pitch but the game was hardly chockfull of skill and finesse. Arsenal had despatched assistant manager Wilf Dixon and ex-Gunner George Male to compile a dossier to find United's weaknesses. They worked out that the United defence had a tendency to bunch together and did not defend the far post during crosses. Brian Talbot opened Arsenal's account from a cross by David Price after a run by Liam Brady. On 43 minutes, Brady crossed and Frank Stapleton headed goal number two for Arsenal. Half time came and went and Arsenal seemed to be cruising to an easy win. Then manager Terry Neill made what is still to some a surprising substitution – he pulled off midfielder Price and sent on defender Steve Walford. The decision upset the balance of the Arsenal side and suddenly Manchester United sniffed a chance. From a free kick Joe Jordan pulled the ball across Arsenal's goal for Gordon McQueen to score and then two minutes later, Sammy McIlroy made it 2-2. It seemed that extra time would be needed as with the 1971 game. Brady said, "When United pulled level I was dreading extra time because I was knackered and our substitute was already on." He spotted Graham Rix on the left side of the pitch and passed to him, Rix took off and crossed the ball. Gary Bailey in goal for United misjudged the cross and Alan Sunderland managed to connect with it with enough force to send it over the goal line and give Arsenal a last-minute victory.

SATURDAY 12 MAY 2001

With Wembley being demolished, the FA Cup Final moved to the Millennium Stadium in Cardiff; the first final to be played outside of England was Arsenal versus Liverpool. Oddly, in a reverse of the 1971 final, Liverpool wore gold and blue and Arsenal played in their usual red (and white). With 72 minutes on the clock, Freddie Ljungberg opened the scoring but two goals by Michael Owen broke Arsenal's heart and the trophy went to Liverpool. The attendance was 72,400.

SATURDAY 13 MAY 1933

Left-back Eddie Hapgood made his England debut against Italy in Rome in a match that ended in a one-all draw. Teammate Cliff Bastin scored England's goal.

WEDNESDAY 14 MAY 1980

Four days after losing to West Ham United in the FA Cup Final, Arsenal lost 5-4 on penalties to Valencia in the European Cup Winners' Cup Final before 40,000 fans at Brussels.

WEDNESDAY 14 MAY 1986

George Graham became manager of Arsenal, after a successful spell in the chair at Millwall. He became one of the club's most successful managers – winning two First Division championships, one FA Cup, one League Cup and one European trophy (European Cup Winners' Cup) – until he was sacked for "financial irregularities".

SATURDAY 15 MAY 1993

The Gunners and the Owls met again at Wembley for the second cup final of the season. This time 79,347 fans watched the two teams play out a one-all draw (after extra time) in the FA Cup Final with Arsenal's solitary goal coming from Ian Wright who was playing with a broken toe. Luckily, he scored with his head. This was the first FA Cup final in which squad numbers had been used, having been trialled in the League Cup final. Players from both clubs used the same numbers for all three matches. The Premier League adopted the system for the following season (see 18 April, 1993, 20 May 1993).

SATURDAY 15 MAY 1993

The official 1993 FA Cup Final song Shouting For The Gunners entered the hit parade. Featuring Tippa Irie and Peter Hunnigale, it spent three weeks on the chart and reached number 34.

SUNDAY 15 MAY 1994

Tony Adams and friends visited the Crown pub in Billericay where instead of watching the FA Cup Final between Manchester United and Chelsea, they enjoyed a stripper called Alison Frost gyrating in a back room.

SATURDAY 15 MAY 2004

Arsenal beat Leicester City 2-1 to complete a season of unbeaten football in the league.

SATURDAY 16 MAY 1925

Manager Leslie Knighton sacked by chairman Sir Henry Norris paving the way for Herbert Chapman to take the hot seat at Highbury.

SATURDAY 16 MAY 1998

Arsenal returned to Wembley for the FA Cup Final, against Newcastle United. Dennis Bergkamp was missing through a hamstring injury but most neutrals still expected Arsenal to win and complete their second Double, in Arsène Wenger's first full season in charge. And so it proved: Marc Overmars and Nicolas Anelka scored Arsenal's goals in the 23rd and 69th minutes respectively before 79,183 fans.

MONDAY 17 MAY 1993

A near full-strength Arsenal lined up against Manchester United for David O'Leary's testimonial game. Twenty-two thousand, one hundred and seventeen turned up to watch a 4-4 draw.

WEDNESDAY 17 MAY 2000

Arsenal played Galatasaray in the Uefa Cup Final at the Parken Stadium, Copenhagen before 38,919 fans. The score at full-time and after extra time was 0-0 and penalties decided the match. Arsenal could not seem to get their goal-scoring act together and Galatasaray won 4-1. It was the first European trophy won by a Turkish club.

SATURDAY 17 MAY 2003

In a repeat of 1978-80, Arsenal returned for their third consecutive FA Cup Final. They faced Southampton. There were 73,726 spectators at the match and, due to poor weather, the game was effectively played indoors. David Seaman, in his last appearance for the club, donned the captain's armband. Sol Campbell did not play after being sent off against Manchester United and Patrick Vieira was missing through a knee injury also obtained in the same match against United. Keown and Luzhny only played after being passed fit on the morning of the game. Arsenal wore their usual red and white strip but as with the game against Liverpool two years earlier, their opponents wore what had been Arsenal's normal away strip of yellow and blue. The game has quickly been forgotten but Robert Pirès scored the winning goal in the 38th minute.

WEDNESDAY 17 MAY 2006

Arsenal appeared in the final of the European Cup (European Champions League), the one international trophy that had eluded them. The match took place at the Stade de France in Paris. After 18 minutes, tragedy struck as Jens Lehmann was sent off for a professional foul on Samuel Eto'o. Arsène Wenger withdrew Robert Pirès, much to the French player's upset, and replaced him with reserve goalie Manuel Almunia who had not played a game in four months. Lehmann was the first player to be sent off in the final. Arsenal scored first in the 37th minute, as Sol Campbell got his head on the end of a Thierry Henry free kick. The rain began to fall and gradually, the 11 men of Barcelona began to make their superior numbers felt and Eto'o equalised in the 76th minute. Four minutes later, substitute Juliano Belletti hit the winner for the Spaniards putting it between Almunia's legs. Thierry Henry said, "They kicked me all over the place but I was the one who got a yellow card. No disrespect to Barcelona but we were the better team when it was 11 v 11." The next day, the referee Terje Hauge admitted that he had made a mistake in sending off Lehmann.

FRIDAY 18 MAY 1990

Steve Morrow made his international debut for Northern Ireland in a one-nil victory over Uruguay.

MONDAY 19 MAY 1958

Jack Crayston resigned as Arsenal manager after a disappointing 18 months in the chair.

THURSDAY 19 MAY 1977

Goalkeeper Manuel Almunia born at Pamplona, Spain. Although he joined Arsenal in 2004 it was not until midway through the 2006-07 season that he made the keeper's position his own.

MONDAY 19 MAY 1980

Midfielder Liam "Chippy" Brady played his final game for Arsenal as the Gunners went down 5-0 to Middlesbrough at Ayresome Park.

FRIDAY 19 MAY 2006

Thierry Henry ended months of speculation about his future by signing a new four-year contract with Arsenal. He said, "At one point it crossed my mind to leave. But I think with my heart and my heart told me to stay. I've never played in Spain and never will. This is my last contract. This is the best country to play football. It's the passion I like. Here you can do your job in the right way – people here respect the players. The way we lost [to Barcelona in the Champions League Final] showed me they are a team with heart and lots of quality. In the past year the fans have been more than amazing, I couldn't let them down." (See 25 June 2007)

THURSDAY 20 MAY 1993

Arsenal and Sheffield Wednesday returned to Wembley for the FA Cup Final replay. Both FA Cup semi-finals were staged at Wembley, so the Gunners and the Owls each played there four times in six weeks – FA Cup semi-final, League Cup Final, FA Cup Final and replay. The replay attracted the smallest crowd (62,267) for an FA Cup Final at Wembley. The kick-off was put back half an hour because a crash on the M1 had delayed thousands of Wednesday fans. It was the first time a Wembley kick-off had not kicked off on time since the White Horse final in 1923. It was also raining heavily. In the early stages, Mark Bright went in roughly on Andy Linighan and broke the Arsenal man's nose. Ian Wright opened the scoring on 34 minutes putting Arsenal ahead as he had done in the first game but after 61 minutes Chris Waddle equalised for Wednesday and that was the way it stayed at 90 minutes. With just a minute of extra time remaining Andy Linighan won the game for Arsenal with a header.

SATURDAY 21 MAY 2005

Arsenal and Manchester United lined up in front of 71,876 fans for the FA Cup. Arsenal wore their usual red and white kit while United played in black shirts and shorts and white stockings. There followed 120 goalless minutes – the first final without goals since 1912. Then the FA Cup was decided on penalties for the first time. José Antonio

Reyes was sent off in the last minute of extra time for fouling Cristiano Ronaldo. When it came to the penalties Jens Lehmann made a brilliant save to defy Paul Scholes and Patrick Vieira put the ball past United's Roy Carroll to win the game for Arsenal. It was Vieira's last kick before leaving Highbury for a new life in Italy with Juventus.

TUESDAY 22 MAY 1990

Having brought David Seaman to Highbury from Queens Park Rangers, George Graham sold John Lukic back to Leeds United after seven years at Highbury for £1,000,000. Seaman had been Lukic's deputy at Elland Road. In 1996 Lukic rejoined Arsenal this time as Seaman's deputy.

THURSDAY 23 MAY 1918

All-rounder Denis Charles Scott Compton born at 20 Alexandra Road, Hendon, Middlesex, the youngest of three children.

SATURDAY 23 MAY 1998

Hot Stuff, the club's official song for the 1998 FA Cup Final, entered the UK charts. Based on Donna Summers' disco smash hit, it was also the most successful Arsenal song spending five weeks on the chart and peaking at number nine.

TUESDAY 23 MAY 2006

Arsène Wenger bought Czech Republic midfielder Tomáš Rosický from Borussia Dortmund for €10million. He has been nicknamed The Little Mozart for his ability to orchestrate play on the field.

SATURDAY 24 MAY 1919

Having played for the Army, big things were expected of inside-forward Daniel Burgess whom Leslie Knighton signed today. However, the promise did not pan out and in three years he played just 13 games.

SUNDAY 24 MAY 2009

Vito Mannone, Arsenal's third choice goalie, made his first team debut against Stoke City at the Emirates as Arsenal won 4-1. Mannone was the 34th player used by Arsène Wenger in 2008-09. On the bench was fourth choice goalie, Polish youth international Wojciech Szczesny, which meant of Arsenal's four goalies two are Polish.

SATURDAY 25 MAY 1929

A year before his retirement William Blyth joined Birmingham City. He joined Woolwich Arsenal in May 1914 three months before the outbreak of the First World War. His career flourished after the war and he was only the fourth Gunner to play more than 300 league games.

WEDNESDAY 25 MAY 1949

During a tour of Brazil, Arsenal played Vasco de Gama in Rio de Janeiro. The home side triumphed 1-0 and their excitable supporters invaded the pitch. As the authorities battled to contain the invasion, a Brazilian policeman accidentally hit Bryn Jones on the head causing injuries so severe that on doctor's advice he decided to retire from football.

FRIDAY 26 MAY 1989

Arsenal won 2-0 at Anfield to win George Graham his first championship as manager – and the club's first since the Double in 1970-71. Graham told his players he would be happy if the half-time score was 0-0 and perhaps unsurprisingly for a Graham side, at half time the score was indeed 0-0. Seven minutes into the second half, Nigel Winterburn crossed and Alan Smith made it 1-0 with a header. In injury time, Lukic threw the ball to Dixon who passed to Alan Smith who found Mickey Thomas who shot past Bruce Grobbelaar to bring the title to Highbury.

WEDNESDAY 27 MAY 1970

One of the many who failed to shine, midfielder Brian Hornsby joined Arsenal as an apprentice, turning professional in September 1971. An England schoolboy international he was unable to hold down a place in the first team and left for Shrewsbury Town in June 1976 after just 26 first team games in five years.

MONDAY 28 MAY 1934

George Allison appointed manager of Arsenal and stayed in the job for thirteen years and three days.

FRIDAY 28 MAY 1999

Defender Oleg Luzhny joined Arsenal from Dynamo Kiev as cover for Lee Dixon. He was unable to displace Dixon from the side and left in the summer of 2003 having played 75 games for Arsenal.

TUESDAY 29 MAY 1990

Martin Hayes sold to Celtic for £650,000 having failed to displace Alan Smith or Paul Merson in the Arsenal front line.

TUESDAY 30 MAY 1995

Seven-goal man Ted Drake died in London aged 82. Drake scored 139 goals in 184 starts giving him an unrivalled strike rate of a goal every 1.3 matches.

TUESDAY 30 MAY 2006

Theo Walcott became England's youngest international – at 17 years and 75 days – playing in a friendly against Hungary at Old Trafford. England won 3-1.

SATURDAY 31 MAY 1890

Having won two trophies in 1889-1890 Royal Arsenal entered a six-a-side competition at the Agricultural Hall, Islington organised by the National Physical Recreation Society. Arsenal won the competition beating London Caledonians 15-7.

SATURDAY 31 MAY 1941

Arsenal lost the Football League War Cup Final replay 2-1 to Preston North End at Ewood Park, Blackburn after drawing the first match three weeks earlier at Wembley.

SATURDAY 31 MAY 1947

George Allison resigned as Arsenal manager, to be replaced by his assistant Tom Whittaker.

SATURDAY 31 MAY 1980

Curly-haired scorer of the winning goal in the 1979 FA Cup Final Alan Sunderland won his only international cap as England beat Australia 2-1 in Sydney.

ARSENAL
On This Day

JUNE

MONDAY 1 JUNE 1953

Inside-left Alex James died in London aged 51 from cancer. He played 261 games. He was recognised for his baggy shorts although he claimed that he only wore them to keep his knees warm.

MONDAY 1 JUNE 2009

Arsenal finished third in the Fair Play League behind Chelsea and Fulham. The club saw off the challenge of Liverpool (4th), Spurs (6th), Manchester United (7th) and bottom club Hull City.

MONDAY 2 JUNE 1947

Tom Whittaker stepped up from the trainer's bench to become manager of Arsenal. He stayed in the job until his premature death.

SUNDAY 2 JUNE 1991

Tottenham-born Gus Caesar joined Cambridge United on a free transfer after nine years and 44 appearances at Highbury. He didn't manage to make the first team and soon moved to Ashton Gate and Bristol City.

THURSDAY 2 JUNE 2005

Ashley Cole was fined £100,000 (later reduced to £75,000) by the Premier League after he had been caught having illegal talks with Chelsea manager José Mourinho and chief executive Peter Kenyon about a move to Stamford Bridge. When the news broke, Cole declared, "I wouldn't play for Arsenal again even for £200,000 a week." (See 18 July 2005)

FRIDAY 3 JUNE 1988

After Gus Caesar's disastrous performance in the League Cup Final, George Graham began to sign centre backs and Steve Bould arrived at Highbury today from Stoke City for £390,000.

TUESDAY 3 JUNE 1997

Keeper Alex Manninger joined Arsenal from Casino Graz as the reserve to David Seaman.

SATURDAY 3 JUNE 2000

'Arsenal Number 1', sang to the tune of 'Mambo No.5' by Lou Bega, reached number 46 in the charts during its one-week stay.

SATURDAY 4 JUNE 1977

Arsenal goalkeeper Alex Manninger born in Salzburg, Austria.

FRIDAY 5 JUNE 1903

Left-back Fred Dwight signed by Harry Bradshaw from Fulham. However, Dwight was unable to break through into the first team and left for Nelson having made just one appearance for the first team.

FRIDAY 6 JUNE 1930

Arsenal boss Herbert Chapman sold centre-half John Butler to Torquay United for £1,000. Butler had signed professional terms with the Gunners in March 1914 only for the First World War to break out five months later. He served in France with the Royal Field Artillery during the conflict. He also played in two wartime matches for Arsenal and scored four times. Back in red after the war, he stayed at the club for a dozen years.

THURSDAY 7 JUNE 1928

Left-half Dave Bowen was born in Nantyffyllon, South Wales. Bowen played 162 games for Arsenal and after nine years at Highbury, he joined Northampton Town in July 1959 where he was player-manager for ten months. He stayed on as manager for a further nine years before moving upstairs to become successively secretary and general manager prior to his retirement in June 1986. From 1964 until 1974, he was part-time manager of Wales.

TUESDAY 8 JUNE 1982

Terry Neill splashed out £500,000 to bring forward Tony Woodcock to Highbury from German side 1. FC Cologne. Woodcock repaid Neill by being the club's top scorer for the next four seasons, his best tally being 21 in 1983-84. An injury and George Graham signalled the end of Woodcock's time at Arsenal and after 68 goals in 169 matches he re-signed for 1. FC Cologne.

MONDAY 9 JUNE 1986

George Graham sold Martin Keown to to Aston Villa for £125,000 after the two men fell out when Keown asked for another £50 a week. He played 22 times for the club.

MONDAY 10 JUNE 1985

Midfielder Brian Talbot sold to Watford for £150,000 after six and a half years at Highbury during which time he played 327 times and scored 49 goals. He had become the first player to play in winning sides in successive FA Cup Finals (Ipswich Town in 1978 and Arsenal the following year).

THURSDAY 11 JUNE 1925

Herbert Chapman appointed Arsenal manager. Under him the club would become the most successful of the 1930s.

MONDAY 11 JUNE 2007

Goalie Łukasz Fabiański, 22, boasted that he would be Arsenal's first-choice keeper in 2007-08. He told an interviewer, "[Jens] Lehmann and [Manuel] Almunia are very good, but I'm not afraid of anyone. I'm confident of my skills. I want to be first choice at Arsenal as much as they do. My message is clear – I'm ready to fight from day one." Fabiański didn't achieve his ambition but stood in for Almunia in 2008-09 when the Spaniard was injured.

THURSDAY 11 JUNE 2009

Keen to extend the merchandising side of football, Arsenal opened their first supporters' shop in the Middle East, in Bahrain city centre.

TUESDAY 12 JUNE 1945

Goalie Pat Jennings born at Newry, County Down. He is probably the only player to have played for Arsenal and the team from the wrong end of the Seven Sisters Road and retained the affection of both sets of supporters.

THURSDAY 12 JUNE 1980

Terry Neill paid £1.25m to sign Clive Allen from Queens Park Rangers. The move made him Britain's sixth million-pound footballer. After a medical, Allen signed a contract, which Neill described as being "for a long time" – the player also received £80,000 as his share of the transfer money. Neill said, "We don't do things lightly here. Our supporters deserve the best and that is what I believe we have given them by buying Clive." Allen left before playing for the first team.

FRIDAY 12 JUNE 2009

Goalie Łukasz Fabiański signed a four-year contract at Arsenal consolidating his place as Manuel Almunia's deputy.

FRIDAY 13 JUNE 1966

Billy Wright was sacked as Arsenal manager after four years without a trophy.

MONDAY 13 JUNE 1983

Defender John Devine joined Norwich on a free transfer after eight and a half years at Highbury. A full-back, he preferred playing on the right and made his debut on Saturday 22 April 1978, in a 3-1 win over Leeds United. He played 111 Arsenal games but never really made a name for himself at the club. Injury blighted his last two years at Highbury and he only played 23 games. In 1981, he married Irish beauty queen Michelle Rocca but they divorced in 1990. Rocca, who hosted the 1988 Eurovision Song Contest, is now the girlfriend of Van Morrison, the singer. Devine was manager of Shelbourne for a short period in 1989.

MONDAY 14 JUNE 1993

Eddie McGoldrick joined Arsenal from Crystal Palace for £850,000. He played 57 times for Arsenal, scoring one goal before leaving for Manchester City in 1996.

THURSDAY 14 JUNE 2001

Arsenal boss Arsène Wenger paid Everton £8million for Francis Jeffers who commented, "It's a massive club, one of the biggest in Europe and for them to be interested in me is magnificent. Playing with world class players I'm definitely looking to improve." Or perhaps not…

THURSDAY 15 JUNE 1995

Bruce Rioch appointed manager of Arsenal. His reign was the shortest in modern times apart from caretaker bosses.

THURSDAY 16 JUNE 1994

6ft 1in Lee Harper began his football career at non-league

Sittingbourne before joining Arsenal for £150,000 today. On 15 March 1997, he made his one and only appearance for the first team in a 2-0 win over Southampton in the Premier League. A few months later, on 9 July 1997, he left Highbury for Loftus Road where he played more than 100 first-team games for Queens Park Rangers who paid £125,000 for him.

TUESDAY 17 JUNE 1997

Arsène Wenger signed a trio of international talent in Marc Overmars, Emmanuel Petit and Gilles Grimandi.

MONDAY 18 JUNE 1979

Midfielder Paul Davis joined Arsenal. In a career spanning 17 years at Highbury Davis represented the Gunners 790 times at all levels. He returned to the Emirates as youth team coach.

MONDAY 19 JUNE 1944

Right-half Herbie Roberts serving with the Royal Fusiliers as a lieutenant died from erysipelas – an acute bacterial infection of the skin – at the age of 39. Tom Whittaker said, "Roberts' genius came from his intelligence and, even more important, he did what he was told."

FRIDAY 19 JUNE 2009

Belgian defender Thomas Vermaelen joined Arsenal from Ajax for an initial fee of €10million (£8.45million), rising to €12million (£10.1million.)

FRIDAY 20 JUNE 1966

The Arsenal board appointed physiotherapist Bertie Mee to the manager's chair. He asked for a let-out clause in his contract that if he was not happy after twelve months he could return to his old job. The clause was never needed.

TUESDAY 20 JUNE 1995

Dennis Bergkamp signed for Arsenal from Internazionale for £7.25million – the first major player brought to the club by Bruce Rioch.

SATURDAY 21 JUNE 1958

George Swindin appointed manager of Arsenal. In his four years in the chair he was unable to bring any trophies to Highbury and saw the team from the wrong end of the Seven Sisters Road win the Double in 1960-61.

WEDNESDAY 22 JUNE 1983

Charlie Nicholas joined Arsenal from Celtic for £750,000. He said, "I regard commercial interests as a bonus as long as they don't affect my game." He quickly made more headlines for his off-pitch activities than what he did in the famous red and white. He dated the beautiful gymnast Suzanne Dando and claimed that he ended the relationship because she liked seeing her face in the tabloids a little too often for his liking! Singer Thereza Bazar from fluffy pop duo Dollar sold a kiss'n'tell about Nicholas, four years her junior, to the *News of the World*. She pointedly noted that although Nicholas had problems scoring on the pitch he had scored a hat-trick with her. In the space of four years, he was twice charged with drink driving. On one occasion, Nicholas tried to disguise his inebriation by driving home at a careful 10mph, zigzagging as he went. He received a three-year ban when he appeared before the magistrate. He was sold to Aberdeen on 7 January 1988 for £400,000.

MONDAY 22 JUNE 2009

Tory MP John Bercow became the first Arsenal supporter to be elected Speaker of the House of Commons.

SATURDAY 23 JUNE 2007

After pledging his future to Arsenal and claiming that he never would play in Spain, striker Thierry Henry signed for Barcelona for €24million (£16million). Henry explained, "Arsenal will be in my blood as well as my heart. I said I was going to be a Gunner for life and I didn't lie because when you are a Gunner you will always be a Gunner." Journalist and Arsenal fan Piers Morgan was less forgiving as he noted in his diary, "Thierry Henry assured me he was 'a Gooner for life'. He even gave me one of his shirts signed to that effect. I subsequently told all my fellow Arsenal fans to relax. 'He wouldn't lie to me,' I insisted. Today, Henry signed for Barcelona. The lying little bastard."

THURSDAY 24 JUNE 1999

German midfielder Stefan Malz joined Arsenal from TSV 1860 Munich. He never managed to hold down a first team place and in the two years before he left he made just half a dozen appearances for the Gunners.

SATURDAY 25 JUNE 1960

Former club captain Charlie Buchan died suddenly of a heart attack while on holiday with his wife at Monte Carlo.

FRIDAY 26 JUNE 1970

Arsenal stalwart Terry Neill left Highbury to become player-manager at Hull City for £40,000.

MONDAY 27 JUNE 2005

Romford, Essex-born 6ft 5in goalkeeper Stuart Taylor left Arsenal and signed for Aston Villa on a four-year deal. He joined ex-Gunner David O'Leary, who was manager of the Villans. Taylor said, "This is all about career progression. It was no good for me to stay at Arsenal. This is a new start. I enjoyed my time at Arsenal but it's time to move on." Taylor left after he found himself behind new signings Jens Lehmann and Manuel Almunia. Taylor made 30 senior appearances for the Gunners.

TUESDAY 28 JUNE 1921

England amateur international inside-left Reg Boreham arrived at Highbury from Wycombe Wanderers. He played 51 times for the Gunners before his contract was terminated.

FRIDAY 29 JUNE 1923

Goalie Ernest Williamson – Arsenal's first post-First World War England international – left the club for Carrow Road and Norwich City. He played 297 games at all levels for Arsenal.

WEDNESDAY 30 JUNE 1999

Silvinho became the first Brazilian to join Arsenal when Arsène Wenger signed him from Corinthians. The Sao Paolo-born midfielder's full name is Silvinho Mendes Campos.

TUESDAY 30 JUNE 2009

Arsenal parted company with eight reserve and youth team players after deciding that they did not have a future at the Emirates. The eight were Portuguese Under-21 international Amaury Bischoff, James Dunne, Portuguese Under-17 international Rui Fonte, Abu Ogogo, Paul Rodgers, Rene Steer, Dutch Under-17 international Vincent van den Berg, Anton Blackwood and Danish youth international Jonas Rasmussen.

ARSENAL
On This Day

JULY

SATURDAY 1 JULY 2006

A player loan agreement expired between Arsenal and Belgian side Koninklijke Sportkring Beveren. The deal began in 2001 and was investigated by *Newsnight* who claimed that a loan of more than €1.5million by Arsenal to the Belgian side which guaranteed their future had been in breach of Fifa regulations. Arsenal said that the money was an interest free loan and has no effect on the administration of the club. The FA and Fifa cleared both clubs of any wrongdoing.

TUESDAY 1 JULY 2008

Farewell to midfielder Mathieu Flamini and goalie Jens Lehmann who left the Emirates. Flamini signed a four-year contract with AC Milan for £4million after Arsène Wenger refused to offer him more than £55,000-a-week. Lehmann who had just won a European Championships runners-up medal joined VfB Stuttgart.

THURSDAY 2 JULY 2009

Chief executive Ivan Gazidis said the Premier League should consider introducing a salary cap for its clubs to encourage financial stability and more even competition throughout the league.

TUESDAY 3 JULY 2001

Sol Campbell signed for Arsenal from Spurs. Of all the players who have played for both clubs, Campbell has probably received more stick than any other. Cries of "Judas" and "Traitor" have echoed around Tottenham when he returned to the club he served so loyally but clad in Arsenal's red and white. He began his career at White Hart Lane in 1990 and spent almost 11 years with Spurs making more than 300 first team appearances before a shock free transfer under the Bosman ruling saw him move to Highbury. During his time with Spurs they had never finished higher than seventh and Campbell had expressed a wish to actually win something at club level. In his first season at Highbury, Campbell won championship and FA Cup winner's medals as Arsenal completed the Double.

THURSDAY 4 JULY 2002

Goalkeeper Alex Manninger "signed" for RCD Espanyol for £960,000. Seven weeks later, Espanyol released Manninger claiming that the transfer had never been completed. Manninger fumed, "It's incredible that [Espanyol] believe they are not in the wrong. I think that very bad things happen in the real world, but in football even more incredible things happen. A club should not treat anyone in this manner, not a junior player, and much less an international player. I can't believe what [Espanyol director, Josep Lluis Marco] said to me on my last day at the club. He is a great actor. He gave me the impression that Espanyol never had the money to pay my transfer and sign me. Moreover, Arsenal will not sit around with their arms folded, and are preparing with Fifa to make Espanyol pay the €1million they owe. I went to Spain because I saw a good opportunity. But Espanyol came close to ending my career." Manninger joined Torino in January 2003.

WEDNESDAY 5 JULY 1978

Arsenal manager Terry Neill signed goalkeeper Paul Barron from Plymouth Argyle for £70,000 as reserve to Pat Jennings. A more than capable keeper, Barron was unable to displace Jennings from between the sticks and played just eight games in two seasons. In 1980, he joined Crystal Palace along with Clive Allen in the deal that brought Kenny Sansom to Highbury. He is currently goalkeeping coach at Newcastle United.

THURSDAY 5 JULY 2001

Arsène Wenger splashed out £6million to bring goalkeeper Richard Wright to Highbury on a five-year contract. Some sources suggest the figure was actually around £2million due to a clause in Wright's contract. The new goalie said, "I can definitely learn from David [Seaman] because he has so much experience and has achieved so much in the game. But I want to play first team football. I will be disappointed if I begin the season on the bench. I'm not taking anything for granted but I feel I can push David Seaman for the number one position. I think it is good to have challenges in life." Arsène Wenger said, "I know picking a goalkeeper for our first game of the season will be a tough decision but I accept that. The great thing about Seaman is that he accepts that as well. David has 15 years of extra knowledge to pass on to Richard and although it is a competitive situation Richard will be able to learn a lot."

THURSDAY 6 JULY 1995

Jimmy Carter left Arsenal for pastures new in the south joining Portsmouth. He had made only 25 league appearances since his £500,000 move from Liverpool in October 1991. He now plays for Arsenal's veterans' side in the Masters Cup Football competition.

MONDAY 7 JULY 1975

In a deal that still puzzles the Arsenal faithful manager Bertie Mee sold Highbury hero Charlie George to Derby County for £90,000.

MONDAY 7 JULY 1997

Arsène Wenger sold Paul Merson to Middlesbrough for £5million. In all Merson played 423 times for Arsenal, scoring 99 goals. He won two championship medals at Highbury as well as FA Cup, League Cup and European Cup Winners' Cup honours.

THURSDAY 8 JULY 1971

Double-winning coach Don Howe left Highbury to become manager of West Bromwich Albion.

SATURDAY 8 JULY 2006

After an unhappy few months Sol Campbell was revealed to have left Arsenal. He made 197 appearances for Arsenal, scoring 11 goals, in all competitions. "It is with a sense of pride, achievement and the desire for a fresh challenge that I depart. I would like to thank Arsène Wenger for everything he has done for me, the world class players that I have been privileged to play alongside and accomplish so much," said Campbell. Arsène Wenger added, "Sol has been a giant for us but we respect his decision to move on and of course, we are very sorry to see him go. His desire and presence have been instrumental to our success over the past five years. Sol was at the heart of our defence and he will take away with him many fantastic memories, which he richly deserves. Winning two Premiership titles, three FA Cups and scoring in the Champions League final against Barcelona will surely be highlights he will treasure. I know that the younger players, who have progressed here over recent times, have benefited hugely from playing alongside Sol."

FRIDAY 9 JULY 1976

Terry Neill became Arsenal's youngest ever manager replacing Bertie Mee after being headhunted by the board.

SUNDAY 10 JULY 1977

During a tour of the Far East and Australia, the players were told to attend a function with officials from Singapore and the British Embassy. After half an hour of chitchat, Macdonald and Hudson walked out. The next day, Terry Neill laid into them telling them that they had embarrassed the club.

TUESDAY 11 JULY 2000

Arsenal signed Edu from Corinthians but he was unable to join the club after it was realised that he was in possession of a fake Portuguese passport.

FRIDAY 12 JULY 1974

Bertie Mee continued the break-up of the Double-winning side selling Ray Kennedy to Liverpool for £180,000.

TUESDAY 12 JULY 1977

On their tour of the Far East and Australia, Arsenal played Red Star Belgrade and lost 2-1 (Malcolm Macdonald scored the goal). The players lost around eight pints of fluid during the match and a local Australian doctor suggested that they replaced the liquid by drinking water or beer. Offering beer as a solution to dehydration was probably not what the club would have liked to hear but the players took the medic at his word. Macdonald said he drank 20 pints and Hudson added a few gin and tonics to his diet.

THURSDAY 12 JULY 2007

Right-back Bacary Sagna signed for Arsenal from Auxerre for an undisclosed fee, thought to have been an initial £6.1m (€9m) rising to £7.45m (€11m).

MONDAY 13 JULY 1998

Another North Bank favourite left the club. Striker Ian Wright signed for West Ham United for £500,000.

THURSDAY 14 JULY 2005

Patrick Vieira left Arsenal to join Juventus. Vieira had played 407 times for Arsenal and scored 34 times.

MONDAY 14 JULY 2008

In a poll conducted by Arsenal.com to find the Gunners' Greatest 50 Players Thierry Henry was voted into first place and Dennis Bergkamp second.

SUNDAY 15 JULY 1979

Assuming that he was nearing the end of his career John Hollins signed for Arsenal from Queen Park Rangers only to find that his career was revitalised and he played 173 games for the Gunners.

TUESDAY 16 JULY 1963

Goalie Bob Wilson signed for Arsenal as an amateur. He played 308 games for Arsenal before his early retirement in May 1974 and was the first England-born player to play for Scotland, having played for England Schoolboys.

THURSDAY 17 JULY 2008

Brazil midfielder Gilberto signed a three-year deal for Greek club Panathinaikos for £1million after six years at Arsenal. Gilberto, who became Greece's highest-paid player, said, "I came to Greece because I have big ambitions, it's very important for me to be able to continue to give my best. I couldn't say no to the offer. After he joined Arsenal from Brazilian club side Atletico Mineiro made 244 appearances for the club and scored 24 goals.

SUNDAY 18 JULY 2004

Goalkeeper Manuel Almunia joined Arsenal. It took him a while to establish himself above Jens Lehmann in the Arsenal hierarchy.

MONDAY 18 JULY 2005

Despite being tapped up by Chelsea, left-back Ashley Cole signed a new contract at Arsenal. Arsène Wenger commented, "If people come to your window and talk to your wife every night, you can't accept it without asking what's happening."

SATURDAY 19 JULY 2008

Arsenal beat Barnet 2-1 in a pre-season friendly, using 24 players. Arsène Wenger substituted the entire team on 46 minutes and eighteen minutes later substituted two of the substitutes bringing on Wojciech Szczesny to replace Vito Mannone in goal and James Dunne for Abu Ogogo.

TUESDAY 20 JULY 1943

Double-winning left back Bob McNab born at Huddersfield. He joined Arsenal in October 1966 and made his England debut two years later. A regular in the team, he played 365 times for Arsenal before he left on a free transfer in the summer of 1975. He had a showbiz bent appearing as a pundit for ITV during the 1970 World Cup, appearing as a footballer in an episode of the sitcom *On The Buses* and his daughter Mercedes is a successful actress in Hollywood. McNab runs a property empire in Los Angeles, California.

THURSDAY 21 JULY 1898

Arsenal manager Tom Whittaker born at East Cavalry Barracks, Aldershot, Hampshire where his father was a sergeant major. Young Tom was raised at Newcastle upon Tyne and joined Arsenal on 11 November 1919 signing professional terms two months later. He stayed with the club until 1956 becoming manager in 1947.

WEDNESDAY 22 JULY 1992

George Graham broke David Rocastle's heart when he sold the midfielder to Leeds United for £2million.

THURSDAY 22 JULY 2004

Mathieu Flamini joined Arsenal on a free transfer much to the annoyance of Marseille manager José Anigo who ranted, "This is a beautiful treason. He used me." Flamini hit back: "This is not a matter of money. I just didn't get on well with the manager and failed to reach an agreement."

SATURDAY 22 JULY 2006

Dennis Bergkamp's testimonial against Ajax was the first match played at the Emirates Stadium. Arsenal won 2-1 and the first half was made up of current Arsenal players with the second half consisting of a team of veterans. Goals came from Thierry Henry and Nwankwo Kanu.

SUNDAY 23 JULY 1865

The man who made Arsenal great Colonel Sir Henry Norris born at 23 Royal Terrace, Kennington, London.

THURSDAY 23 JULY 1942

Former Arsenal midfielder and Surrey batsman Andrew Ducat died of a heart attack while batting for Surrey Home Guard against Sussex Home Guard at Lord's. He was one of the few people to have represented England at international level at both football and cricket. He was 56 and is the only person in history to have died during a match at Lord's.

MONDAY 23 JULY 2007

The Arsenal Scotland Supporters Club unveiled a plaque to club founder David Danskin, near his birthplace in Burntisland, Fife.

WEDNESDAY 24 JULY 2002

After a rather disastrous one-year spell at Highbury during which he played a dozen games, Richard Wright joined Everton for £3,500,000.

SUNDAY 24 JULY 1977

On their tour of the Far East and Australia, Arsenal lost 3-2 to Celtic at the Sydney Cricket Ground. Manager Terry Neill banned the players from drinking but they ignored him. George Armstrong joined Alan Hudson and Malcolm Macdonald on a drinking spree. On their return to the hotel, Arsenal chairman Denis Hill-Wood bought Macdonald a gin and tonic in the hotel bar. Then Macdonald and Hudson both took sleeping pills and went to bed. Unfortunately, Neill had arranged a training session and sent club captain Pat Rice to their rooms to rouse the two sleeping players. It was too much for Neill and he sent Hudson and Macdonald home. Although George Armstrong asked to be sent home, Neill refused. Liam Brady later admitted that at least ten other players should also have been sent home for they had committed the same "offence". Back home in England Hudson never played for Arsenal again although Malcolm Macdonald and Terry Neill made their peace. In October 1978, Hudson was sold to Seattle Sounders for £100,000, half the money Terry Neill had paid for him in December 1976.

MONDAY 25 JULY 1983

Two goalies arrived at Arsenal twenty years apart. In 1983 John Lukic signed for the Gunners from Leeds United in what would be his first spell at Highbury. Twenty years later, Jens Lehmann joined Arsenal from Borussia Dortmund.

THURSDAY 26 JULY 1973

Golden boy turned fallen idle Peter Marinello left Highbury for Portsmouth for £80,000. In his time at the Marble Halls he played 151 games in all competitions. He later said, "At first, I found everything so different at Highbury from what I was used to, but I really regret not staying at Arsenal. I could see the chance to make a proper breakthrough with the Double-winning team splitting up, but I was just too impulsive back then and went after the money."

THURSDAY 27 JULY 2006

The clock removed from the South Bank aka the Clock End at Highbury. It has been installed at the Emirates facing the Clock End Bridge. It took four people nine hours and a 25-ton crane to put the clock in place.

SUNDAY 28 JULY 2002

Arsenal signed Brazilian World Cup winner Gilberto Silva from Atletico Mineiro for a reported fee of £4.5million. The player said, "I am delighted to be joining Arsenal. They are the champions of England and have a squad full of world-class international footballers. I am really looking forward to living to London and playing for one of the best teams in Europe."

MONDAY 28 JULY 2008

Arsenal beat Burgenland XI 10-2 in a pre-season friendly with Nicklas Bendtner scoring four goals in the first half (before he was substituted at half-time) and Carlos Vela scoring a hat-trick.

THURSDAY 29 JULY 1976

New Arsenal manager Terry Neill showed he meant business when he paid Newcastle United a fee of £333,333 for centre forward Malcolm Macdonald.

MONDAY 30 JULY 1934

Arsenal's most influential chairman Colonel Sir Henry Norris died at his home, Sirron Lodge, Barnes Common, London five years after he had been forced to relinquish control of the club.

THURSDAY 31 JULY 2008

The man with the magic sponge Gary Lewin left Arsenal after new England boss Fabio Capello wanted a full-time physio in his England set-up. A bigger pay packet and the chance to travel the world observing new techniques for coping with injuries provided too much of a lure for Lewin who had been with Arsenal since 1980 and first team physio since 1986 replacing Roy Johnson.

ARSENAL
On This Day

AUGUST

FRIDAY 1 AUGUST 1980

In a move that upset the Highbury faithful Liam Brady was sold to Juventus for £514,000. Chippy made more than 200 appearances for the Gunners in seven years at Highbury.

SUNDAY 1 AUGUST 1982

Forward Lee Chapman signed for Arsenal for £500,000 from Stoke City with the fee set by a tribunal.

TUESDAY 1 AUGUST 2006

Defender Armand Traoré joined the club from AS Monaco. He played just three Premier League games for the Gunners before being loaned to Portsmouth for the 2008-09 season where he played 17 times and netted once.

THURSDAY 2 AUGUST 1934

Arsenal's influential former chairman Colonel Sir Henry Norris buried in East Sheen cemetery.

WEDNESDAY 2 AUGUST 1978

Paul Barron made his debut against Manchester City. He was one of two keepers that goalkeeping coach Bob Wilson later said he was disappointed with, because he did not achieve as much as he could have.

TUESDAY 3 AUGUST 1999

Arsène Wenger bought French forward Thierry Henry for £10million from Italian side Juventus. It was the second time in their careers that Wenger had managed Henry, having previously been the boss at AS Monaco.

WEDNESDAY 4 AUGUST 1948

Club founder David Danskin died, aged 85, in a hospice at Warwick. He was buried in London Road Cemetery in Coventry, beside his first wife, Georgina.

MONDAY 4 AUGUST 2003

French left-back Gaël Clichy joined the club from AS Cannes for a fee of £250,000.

WEDNESDAY 5 AUGUST 1998

Arsène Wenger bought Nelson Vivas, the Argentinian full-back, from Lugano.

TUESDAY 6 AUGUST 2008

Arsenal beat Huddersfield Town 2-1 before 19,044 fans at the Galpharm Stadium to win the Herbert Chapman Trophy. Arsenal presented Huddersfield with a copy of the bust of the man who took both teams to three consecutive First Division titles in commemoration of Huddersfield's centenary.

SATURDAY 7 AUGUST 1993

Manchester United won the 71st FA Charity Shield beating Arsenal 5-4 at Wembley on penalties after the match finished at 1–1 after 90 minutes.

WEDNESDAY 8 AUGUST 2001

Heroin addict Paul Vaessen found dead in his bathroom in Henbury, Bristol, a large amount of drugs in his bloodstream. He was 39.

SUNDAY 8 AUGUST 2004

Playing in all-blue Arsenal beat Manchester United 3-1 at Millennium Stadium, Cardiff to win the 83rd FA Charity/Community Shield. Arsenal's goals came from Gilberto Silva, José Antonio Reyes and an own goal from Mikaël Silvestre who would sign for Arsenal on 20 August 2008. Oddly, Jérémie Aliadière came on as a substitute for Dennis Bergkamp and then Gaël Clichy replaced him six minutes later after injuring his knee.

SATURDAY 9 AUGUST 1969

Arsenal made a minor kit alteration. Out went the blue and white -hooped stockings for red socks with a white turnover. They stayed until the start of the 1982-83 season when red and blue hooped stockings were introduced.

TUESDAY 9 AUGUST 1977

Defender Mikaël Silvestre – who joined Arsenal from Manchester United in 2008 – was born at Chambray-les-Tours, France.

SATURDAY 10 AUGUST 1991

The one that got away? Andy Cole made his last appearance in an Arsenal shirt when he came on as a substitute in the Charity Shield against Spurs. The match ended in a goalless draw and the two teams shared the trophy.

TUESDAY 10 AUGUST 2004

Flop Francis Jeffers sold to Charlton Athletic for £2.6million. Three years earlier, he had cost Arsène Wenger £8million.

THURSDAY 11 AUGUST 1977

Assuming that he was past his best Spurs sold legendary goalkeeper Pat Jennings to Arsenal. He did not receive a signing-on fee but a four-year contract worth £80,000.

SUNDAY 11 AUGUST 2002

A debut goal from Gilberto won the FA Charity/Community Shield for Arsenal for the fourteenth time. The opponents were Liverpool who had been Premier League runners-up.

FRIDAY 12 AUGUST 1949

Arsenal played Middlesex CCC in a benefit match for Denis Compton.

TUESDAY 12 AUGUST 1980

Clive Allen sold in a deal that saw left-back Kenny Sansom come to Highbury and Allen and reserve goalie Paul Barron sold to Crystal Palace. Allen had only been at the club for two months and had played three friendlies for Arsenal.

FRIDAY 12 AUGUST 1994

Ten years after he joined Arsenal, reserve goalie Alan Miller left signing for Middlesbrough for £500,000. He retired aged 33 because of a back injury.

MONDAY 12 AUGUST 1996

Stewart Houston began his second stint as caretaker manager following the sacking of Bruce Rioch. Realising he was not going to get the job, apparently under any circumstances, he left Arsenal to become manager at Queens Park Rangers and, in a role reversal, appointed Rioch as his assistant.

WEDNESDAY 13 AUGUST 2008

Aaron Ramsey made his debut for Arsenal (as an 84th minute substitute for Theo Walcott) in the first leg of the Champions League, Third Qualifying Round 2-0 win against FC Twente played at Gelredome, Arnhem because the home team's ground was being renovated.

SATURDAY 14 AUGUST 1999

Luis Boa Morte made his last appearance for Arsenal as a second half substitute away to Sunderland. He made just 25 first team appearances before he went to Southampton this month for £500,000.

SUNDAY 14 AUGUST 2005

Arsenal played Newcastle United in the opening game of the last season at Highbury and won 2-0. It was the season that Arsenal wore the redcurrant shirts.

SATURDAY 15 AUGUST 1992

Arsenal played their first match in the Premier League at home to Norwich City. The Gunners lost 4-2 with goals scored by Steve Bould and Kevin Campbell.

SATURDAY 16 AUGUST 1975

Centre-half David O'Leary made his league debut against Burnley at Turf Moor. In total, O'Leary played for Arsenal 1,005 times at league, FA Cup, League Cup, European, friendly, tour, Football Combination, South East Counties, and youth levels. He was also capped 68 times by the Republic of Ireland.

SATURDAY 16 AUGUST 1980

Kenny Sansom made his debut for Arsenal against West Bromwich Albion and appeared in every game that season and the next. He is Arsenal's most capped England player winning 77 (of 86) caps while at Highbury.

SATURDAY 16 AUGUST 2008

Samir Nasri made his Premier League debut for Arsenal and scored in the 1-0 win against West Bromwich Albion at the Emirates before a crowd of 60,071.

TUESDAY 17 AUGUST 1909

Arsenal hard man Wilf Copping born. Nicknamed Iron Head because of his tenacity on the pitch, he was signed by Arsenal in June 1934 for £8,000, as a replacement for Bob John. He had three match day superstitions – he put his left boot on first; he was sixth in the line-up and he never shaved on match days.

WEDNESDAY 17 AUGUST 1977

Arsenal's leading goalscorer Thierry Henry born in Paris. He scored 174 goals in 257 appearances.

SATURDAY 18 AUGUST 2001

Former Spurs player Sol Campbell made his Arsenal debut away at Middlesbrough in a game that the Gunners won 4-0.

SATURDAY 19 AUGUST 1961

Laurie Brown made his debut against Burnley in a 2-2 draw at Highbury. Arsenal converted him into a centre-half and he played more than 100 games for the Gunners, the last being a 4-1 thrashing of Birmingham City at St Andrew's on 28 December 1963. Two months later, in February 1964, after Arsenal had signed Ian Ure, Brown joined Spurs for a fee of £40,000. By coincidence, his first match for Spurs, on 22 February 1964, was against Arsenal and he nearly scored as Spurs won 3-1.

SATURDAY 19 AUGUST 1978

Arsenal's first Australian John Kosmina played his only game at senior level coming on as a substitute against Leeds United. He returned to Australia in May 1979.

SATURDAY 19 AUGUST 1995

Dennis Bergkamp made his debut for Arsenal against Middlesbrough in a 1-1 draw at Highbury.

SOL CAMPBELL MADE HIS LEAGUE DEBUT FOR ARSENAL ON 18 AUGUST 2001

SATURDAY 19 AUGUST 2006

The first league match played at the Emirates, against Aston Villa. The game ended 1-1 and Gilberto Silva scored Arsenal's goal.

SATURDAY 20 AUGUST 1949

Arsenal's caretaker manager on two separate occasions Stewart Houston born at Dunoon. He took over after the sackings of George Graham and Bruce Rioch and despite leading the Gunners to a European Cup final was never in the running for the job full-time. In August 2008 Houston was back at the club working as a scout.

SATURDAY 20 AUGUST 1977

Pat Jennings made his debut for Arsenal as the Gunners lost 1-0 to Ipswich Town.

WEDNESDAY 20 AUGUST 2008

French defender Mikaël Silvestre joined Arsenal, eleven days after his 31st birthday on a two-year deal from Manchester United for an undisclosed fee. He had made 361 appearances for the Red Devils, scoring 10 goals.

SATURDAY 21 AUGUST 1976

Centre forward Malcolm Macdonald made his Division 1 debut for Arsenal at home to Bristol City. Having signed from Newcastle United for £333,333, he boasted, "There is no way I will not be on the score sheet on Saturday." Arsenal lost 1-0.

FRIDAY 21 AUGUST 1981

Malcolm Macdonald's former striking partner Frank Stapleton sold to Manchester United for £900,000.

SATURDAY 22 AUGUST 1964

Liverpool's 3-2 win over Arsenal at Anfield was the first (and only) game featured on the first episode of *Match of the Day*.

SUNDAY 22 AUGUST 1999

Davor Šuker made his league debut as a substitute in the 2-1 home defeat by Manchester United.

SATURDAY 23 AUGUST 1997

Luis Boa Morte made his debut as a sub at Southampton.One of Arsène Wenger's earliest signings (for £1.75m), Boa Morte played just 25 games before joining Southampton in August 1999 for £500,000.

WEDNESDAY 23 AUGUST 2006

Theo Walcott became the youngest player to represent Arsenal in Europe when he played in the home leg of the third qualifying round match of the European Champions League against Dinamo Zagreb. He was 17 years and 129 days old. He was also the youngest Arsenal player to be booked in a European game when he took a shot after the referee had blown his whistle.

THURSDAY 24 AUGUST 1967

Midfielder Michael Thomas born in Lambeth. He played 208 games for Arsenal but none more important than the one against Liverpool in May 1989 when he scored the goal that clinched the championship.

SATURDAY 25 AUGUST 1928

Arsenal and Chelsea became the first teams to wear numbers on their backs in a league match against Sheffield Wednesday and Swansea Town respectively.The system that day (until 1939) used numbers 1-22.

WEDNESDAY 25 AUGUST 2004

Arsenal beat Blackburn Rovers 3-0 at Highbury thanks to goals from Thierry Henry, Cesc Fàbregas and José Antonio Reyes. The victory broke Nottingham Forest's record of 42 league games unbeaten.

SATURDAY 26 AUGUST 2000

French international striker Sylvain Wiltord signed for Arsenal from Bordeaux for a then club-record fee of £13million. He played 104 games scoring 32 goals before he joined Lyon in 2004. He was placed 33rd in a vote to find the top 50 Arsenal players ever.

SATURDAY 27 AUGUST 1938

Bryn Jones scored on his debut against Portsmouth. He also found the net in two of his next games. However, the goals dried up and he was only to get one more before the end of the season.

WEDNESDAY 27 AUGUST 1997

Dennis Bergkamp hit a hat-trick as Arsenal drew 3-3 with Leicester City at Filbert Street.

WEDNESDAY 27 AUGUST 2008

Samir Nasri made his Champions League debut for Arsenal and scored in the 4-0 win (aggregate 6-0) over FC Twente of Holland.

TUESDAY 28 AUGUST 1928

A clock measuring almost 8½ feet across was placed on the North Bank at Highbury. In 1935 it was moved to the opposite end of the ground then known as the College End. Originally the clock gave fans a 45-minute countdown but the Football League made Arsenal change it to an ordinary timepiece.

SATURDAY 28 AUGUST 1982

Lee Chapman made his Arsenal debut against his old club, Stoke City, when Arsenal lost 2-1 at the Victoria Ground. Chapman was injured in training and became unhappy at Highbury wanting to leave.

SATURDAY 28 AUGUST 1993

Ian Wright entered the UK pop charts with his song 'Do The Wright Thing', which peaked at 43 during its two-week stay.

SATURDAY 29 AUGUST 1925

Arsenal lost 1-0 at home to Spurs in the first game of the 1925-26 season, before 53,183 fans at Highbury. The match was to have been a benefit for manager Leslie Knighton or so he claimed and then chairman Sir Henry Norris sacked him before the start of the season to avoid handing over the gate takings – in those days a regular match was declared a benefit rather than a specially arranged fixture. However, Arsenal's poor form the previous season may have weighed more heavily on the chairman's mind. It was instead the first match for Herbert Chapman and also marked the debut of striker Charles Buchan who had been made club captain.

SATURDAY 29 AUGUST 1987

Alan Smith scored his first goal for Arsenal against Portsmouth, two weeks after he made his debut in a 2-1 home defeat against Liverpool.

ALAN SMITH GOT HIS FIRST ARSENAL GOAL IN A 6-0 WIN OVER PORTSMOUTH ON 29 AUGUST 1987

SATURDAY 30 AUGUST 1930

Gerrit Keizer, the first foreign player to play for Arsenal, made his debut in the 4-1 victory against Blackpool at Bloomfield Road. He kept goal for the first dozen games that season. On Saturdays, he would play for Arsenal and then fly back to Holland that night to play for Ajax the next day earning him the nickname The Flying Dutchman. Arsenal's other keepers Charlie Preedy and Bill Harper kept him on his toes and Herbert Chapman eventually tired of the young Dutchman. He dropped Keizer in October and never picked him for the first team again. In July 1931, Keizer moved to Charlton Athletic. He continued to shuttle between London and Amsterdam ostensibly bringing football kits with him. In 1947, Dutch customs officers discovered that he was also importing British bank notes, then an offence. He was fined 30,000 guilders and given a six-month prison sentence. Out of jail, he started a successful greengrocery business and in 1955 became a director of Ajax. He died on 5 December 1980.

SATURDAY 31 AUGUST 1963

Goalie Jack McClelland was injured after 22 minutes of a match against Leicester City with the Gunners trailing 2-0. Centre-forward Joe Baker volunteered to go in goal but despite his best efforts the boys from Filbert Street put another five past him and the Gunners went down 7-2.

THURSDAY 31 AUGUST 2006

Defender William Gallas joined Arsenal from Chelsea in the deal that took disgruntled left-back Ashley Cole to the west London club. In addition, Chelsea paid Arsenal £5million. Chelsea had illegally tapped Cole up in January 2005 and despite his apparent desire to leave Highbury the defender had signed a new contract.

FRIDAY 31 AUGUST 2007

Midfielder Lassana Diarra joined Arsenal on transfer deadline day also from Chelsea for an undisclosed fee. Diarra spent just five months at the Emirates, unhappy that he was not getting more first team action. In January 2008, he joined Portsmouth for a reported fee of around £5million.

ARSENAL
On This Day

SEPTEMBER

SATURDAY 1 SEPTEMBER 1934

Ted Drake and Ray Bowden scored hat-tricks as Arsenal beat Liverpool 8-1 at Highbury. Jack Crayston scored his first goal at Highbury. The season ended in Arsenal's third consecutive league title. Before the match kicked off the band played 21 Today as it was almost 21 years to the day that Woolwich Arsenal played their first match at Highbury.

SATURDAY 2 SEPTEMBER 1893

The first match played by Woolwich Arsenal in the Football League against Newcastle United at the Manor Ground, Plumstead, before a crowd of 10,000. At one stage Woolwich Arsenal were leading 2-0 with goals from Walter Shaw and Arthur Elliott but in the last 15 minutes Newcastle pulled two back to earn a draw.

WEDNESDAY 2 SEPTEMBER 1908

Woolwich Arsenal played their first match under manager George Morrell – and lost 4-0 at home to Everton.

SATURDAY 3 SEPTEMBER 1904

Arsenal played their first match in the First Division – and lost 3-0 to Newcastle United.

THURSDAY 3 SEPTEMBER 1936

Goalkeeper George Swindin made his debut against Brentford in a game that Arsenal lost 2-0. Swindin kept Alex Wilson out of the side (he made just two Division 1 appearances) and competed for the number one jersey with Frank Boulton.

SATURDAY 3 SEPTEMBER 1994

Former manager Sir Billy Wright died aged 70 of stomach cancer.

WEDNESDAY 4 SEPTEMBER 1946

First Division football returned to Highbury and Arsenal lost 3-1 to Blackburn Rovers. Reg Lewis got the solitary goal for the Gunners.

TUESDAY 4 SEPTEMBER 1979

Arsenal achieved their biggest ever winning margin in the League

Cup beating Leeds United 7-0 at Highbury in the second round replay. Goals from Alan Sunderland (a hat-trick) and two penalties from Liam Brady plus one each from Sammy Nelson and Frank Stapleton settled the tie in the Gunners' favour.

SATURDAY 5 SEPTEMBER 1970

Geordie Armstrong hit the back of the net twice as Arsenal beat Spurs 2-0 at Highbury. That season Arsenal did two Doubles – winning the league title and FA Cup and beating Spurs home and at White Hart Lane.

WEDNESDAY 6 SEPTEMBER 1905

Morris Bates who played 73 first-team matches for Royal Arsenal becoming club captain and leading the team to their first trophies, the Kent Senior Cup and London Charity Cup in 1890 died aged 41 at Woolwich, London from tuberculosis.

SATURDAY 6 SEPTEMBER 1913

The first match played at Highbury against Leicester Fosse in front of 20,000 fans. Leicester Fosse's Tommy Benfield scored the first goal at the new stadium but George Jobey equalised to score the first Arsenal goal. A late penalty from Archibald Devine meant the Gunners ran out 2-1 winners. However, the pitch had not been finished and had a distinctive slope. There was no warm water in the dressing rooms and when Jobey was injured, he had to be taken to the dressing room on a milk cart.

FRIDAY 7 SEPTEMBER 1945

Arsenal hard man Peter Storey born at Farnham, Surrey. He joined the Gunners as an apprentice in 1961 and was at the club for 16 years before his former teammate and then manager Terry Neill sold him to Fulham for £10,000. He played 501 times for Arsenal, making him the club's eighth-leading player in terms of appearances. Teammate Alan Hudson said, "Before a game his eyes would become fixated on the walls, or the ceiling. You'd look at the eyes and think, 'Oh my God, what's in his head?' His expression was so eerie. It was like looking at Hannibal Lecter in *The Silence of the Lambs*."

FRIDAY 7 SEPTEMBER 2007

Arsène Wenger signed a contract extension – thought to be worth £4million a year – that will keep him at the club until 2011. He said, "My heart is tied to this football club. It has deep-seated roots and a tremendous heritage. It is my aim to uphold these values and help create new history for future generations. Arsenal is the club of my life. I have been entrusted with complete freedom to implement and execute my plans on what will make the team successful. That means I have a responsibility to the fans to deliver silverware and also a responsibility to the players to help turn our potential into prizes."

TUESDAY 8 SEPTEMBER 1970

Arsenal drew 0-0 with Ipswich Town at Portman Road in the second round of the League Cup before winning the replay at Highbury 4-0.

SATURDAY 8 SEPTEMBER 1984

Arsenal beat Liverpool 3-1 at Highbury to lead Division One for the first time since 1972.

SATURDAY 9 SEPTEMBER 1893

Woolwich Arsenal lost 3-2 in their first away league match (against Notts County) with the goals scored by Arthur Elliott and Walter Shaw.

SATURDAY 10 SEPTEMBER 1904

Arsenal played their first home match in the First Division – a 0-0 draw against Preston North End.

WEDNESDAY 10 SEPTEMBER 2008

Theo Walcott became the youngest player to score a hat-trick for England in the 4-1 win over Croatia at the Maksimir Stadium in Zagreb.

MONDAY 11 SEPTEMBER 1893

Woolwich Arsenal won their first match in the Football League and John Heath scored the club's first hat-trick in the third league (a 4-0 victory against Walsall Town Swifts).

THURSDAY 11 SEPTEMBER 2003

Midfielder Cesc Fàbregas joined Arsenal from Barcelona.

SATURDAY 12 SEPTEMBER 1998

Arsène Wenger signed Freddie Ljungberg for £3million, having only seen him on television playing for Sweden against England. Ljungberg more than lived up to Wenger's expectations, even scoring on his debut as a substitute in a 3-0 win against Manchester United on Sunday 20 September 1998. He went on to play more than 300 games for the club before joining West Ham on 23 July 2007.

TUESDAY 13 SEPTEMBER 1966

Arsenal played their first League Cup match at home to Gillingham. Tommy Baldwin scored Arsenal's goal in a 1-1 draw.

SATURDAY 13 SEPTEMBER 1997

Ian Wright broke Cliff Bastin's goal-scoring record with a hat-trick against Bolton Wanderers.

SATURDAY 13 SEPTEMBER 2008

Jack Wilshere became Arsenal's youngest player when he appeared as a substitute (replacing Robin van Persie in the 81st minute) in the 4-0 Premier League win over Blackburn Rovers at the Emirates. Wilshere was just 16 years, 8 months and 12 days old.

SATURDAY 14 SEPTEMBER 1996

Tony Adams publicly admitted that he was an alcoholic. It was thanks to the regime introduced by Arsène Wenger who joined the club shortly after that Adams extended his career and became the only player in English football history to have captained a league-winning team in three different decades.

WEDNESDAY 15 SEPTEMBER 1971

Arsenal played their first game in the European Cup and beat Strømsgodset IF from Norway 3-1 away before winning the home leg 4-0.

THURSDAY 15 SEPTEMBER 1994

Ian Wright scored against Omonia Nicosia in the European Cup Winners' Cup to begin a run of scoring that lasted for 12 games (see 23 November 1994).

THURSDAY 16 SEPTEMBER 1937

Arsenal v Arsenal Reserves became the first match to be broadcast live on television.

TUESDAY 16 SEPTEMBER 1969

Rookie goalie Malcolm Webster, who turned professional in January 1968, made his debut for Arsenal in the home derby against Spurs, which the Gunners lost 3-2.

WEDNESDAY 16 SEPTEMBER 1970

Arsenal drew two-all with Lazio at the Stadio Olimpico in a bad-tempered first leg of the European Fairs Cup first round. After the match the two teams were wary of each other at the formal banquet. Sammy Nelson and Ray Kennedy went outside to get some fresh air where they encountered Lazio's burly centre half and a fight broke out which was joined by Lazio supporters who were outside the restaurant. Bob Wilson ran in to announce the fight and Arsenal captain Frank McLintock, reserve Jackie Carmichael and Eddie Kelly – Scots all – went outside to get stuck in. McLintock later said he remembered seeing Peter Marinello flying through the air over a parked car. The fight eventually broke up and Arsenal won the second leg 2-0.

SATURDAY 16 SEPTEMBER 1972

Arsenal were playing host to Liverpool at Highbury when linesman Dennis Drewitt was injured. TV presenter Jimmy Hill came down from the commentary box and ran the line for the rest of the match, which ended goalless.

MONDAY 16 SEPTEMBER 1996

Irish former right-back Pat Rice became manager of Arsenal for a fortnight while the club awaited the arrival of Arsène Wenger at Highbury after the board sacked Bruce Rioch.

WEDNESDAY 16 SEPTEMBER 1998

Arsenal played their first match in the European Champions League away to RC Lens. The Gunners drew 1-1 and Marc Overmars scored.

SATURDAY 17 SEPTEMBER 1988

During a televised game against Southampton Arsenal's loyal servant Paul Davis punched Glen Cockerill breaking his jaw. Davis was fined £3,000 and banned for nine games after he was found guilty by television. Neither the referee nor either of his linesmen had seen the incident.

WEDNESDAY 18 SEPTEMBER 1991

Arsenal achieved their biggest ever winning margin in the European Cup beating FK Austria 6-1 at Highbury in the first leg of the first round. Alan Smith hit four but Arsenal lost the second leg 1-0.

SATURDAY 18 SEPTEMBER 1999

Thierry Henry scored his first goal for Arsenal. It was the only goal of the game in a match against Southampton at The Dell.

WEDNESDAY 19 SEPTEMBER 1951

Arsenal played their first match under floodlights at Highbury – a friendly against Hapoel Tel Aviv. The Gunners triumphed 6-1.

SATURDAY 20 SEPTEMBER 1980

Goalkeeper George Wood made his debut in the 2-1 league defeat to Middlesbrough.

SATURDAY 21 SEPTEMBER 1946

Reg Lewis failed to score for the Gunners for the first time in the 1946-47 season – in the seventh match. In the first seventeen matches of the season he hit the back of the net in thirteen of them totalling seventeen goals.

THURSDAY 21 SEPTEMBER 2006

Ashley Cole published his non-best-selling autobiography, *My Defence*, and attacked Arsenal: "When I heard the figure of £55k I nearly swerved off the road, I yelled down the phone, 'He's taking the piss Jonathan [Barnett, Cole's agent].' I was so incensed, I was trembling with anger." The cause of this fury was Arsène Wenger's refusal to pay Cole £60,000 a week. Arsenal fans nicknamed him Cashley Cole.

TUESDAY 22 SEPTEMBER 1891

Charles Murray Buchan (1891–1960), footballer and journalist, was born at 151 Reidhaven Road, Plumstead, London.

SATURDAY 23 SEPTEMBER 1922

Arsenal beat Spurs 2-1 at White Hart Lane in a match so ill-tempered – two players were sent off – that an FA Commission of Inquiry was summoned to investigate and Spurs were warned that their ground would be closed if there was a repeat of the crowd violence. In a masterly understatement *The Times* man reported, "It was a not a satisfactory game from any point of view.

SATURDAY 23 SEPTEMBER 1995

Dennis Bergkamp scored his first goal for Arsenal. In fact, he hit two against Southampton in a 4-2 win at Highbury.

SATURDAY 24 SEPTEMBER 1904

Charlie Satterthwaite scored Arsenal's first goal in the First Division – against Wolves. Arsenal won 2-0 but it was the fourth match of the season and the Gunners had lost two of their first three matches.

THURSDAY 24 SEPTEMBER 1908

Left-back Eddie Hapgood born at 4 Clark's Buildings, Union Road, Bristol, the ninth of ten children. His first job was a milkman working for his brother-in-law and he played in local leagues before joining Kettering Town after Bristol Rovers turned him down. He joined Arsenal in 1927 becoming captain three years later. To supplement his wages at Arsenal he advertised chocolate and men's fashions. Unable to continue in football after his retirement, he became warden of a YMCA hostel for apprentices at the atomic energy research establishment, Harwell.

THURSDAY 24 SEPTEMBER 1998

Coach, chief scout and caretaker manager Steve Burtenshaw fined £7,500 and £2,500 costs by the Football Association for his part in the bungs scandal that saw George Graham sacked. In 1992 he had received £35,000 from agent Rune Hauge following Danish midfielder John Jensen's move from Brondby to Arsenal. Burtenshaw stayed at the club until Bruce Rioch was sacked on 12 August 1996.

WEDNESDAY 24 SEPTEMBER 2003

Six Arsenal players and two Manchester United players charged and one warned by the Football Association for their behaviour at the 0-0 draw at Old Trafford on 21 September 2003. Arsenal were also charged with failing to control their players. Lauren received a £40,000 fine and a four-match suspension. Martin Keown was suspended for three games and fined £20,000. Patrick Vieira was banned for one game and fined £20,000; Ray Parlour also for one match but with a £10,000 fine while Ashley Cole was only fined, albeit £10,000.

WEDNESDAY 25 SEPTEMBER 1963

Arsenal played their first away match in European competition against Staevnet (Denmark) in the Inter-Cities Fairs Cup. Arsenal won 7-1 with Geoff Strong 3, Joe Baker 3, and Johnny MacLeod hitting the net.

WEDNESDAY 25 SEPTEMBER 1991

Ian Wright scored his first goal for Arsenal in a 1-1 League Cup match at Leicester City's Filbert Street.

MONDAY 26 SEPTEMBER 1938

Arsenal won the FA Charity Shield, beating Preston North End 2-1 at Highbury with Ted Drake scoring both.

WEDNESDAY 27 SEPTEMBER 1978

Arsenal achieved their biggest ever winning margin in the Uefa Cup beating Lokomotiv Leipzig 4-1 away in East Germany in the second leg of the first round having already won 3-0 at Highbury. It also marked the debut of 16-year-old Paul Vaessen.

TUESDAY 28 SEPTEMBER 1965

Alan Skirton became Arsenal's first substitute when he replaced Jon Sammels in a 1-1 draw at home to Northampton Town.

SATURDAY 28 SEPTEMBER 1985

David Rocastle made his debut for Arsenal in a 0-0 draw at Highbury against Newcastle United.

SATURDAY 29 SEPTEMBER 2001

Twenty-three-year-old goalie Richard Wright made his first-team debut against Derby County.

SATURDAY 30 SEPTEMBER 1893

Woolwich Arsenal conceded six goals in the Football League for the first time. They lost 6–0 at St James' Park against Newcastle United.

FRIDAY 30 SEPTEMBER 1966

George "Stroller" Graham signed for Arsenal from Chelsea in a swap for Tommy Baldwin and £50,000.

FRIDAY 30 SEPTEMBER 2005

Goalie Graham Stack cleared by a jury of raping a 22-year-old law student at his flat in Beckenham, Kent, after they met in Trap nightclub in Wardour Street, just off London's Oxford Street.

ARSENAL
On This Day

OCTOBER

SATURDAY 1 OCTOBER 1966

The day after he signed for Arsenal George Graham scored on his debut but could not prevent Leicester City winning 4-2 at Highbury.

WEDNESDAY 1 OCTOBER 1969

After Bob Wilson broke his arm Bertie Mee was not confident that rookie goalkeeper Malcolm Webster could fill the role between the sticks so he signed Geoff Barnett from Everton for £35,000. Barnett made his debut three days later but as soon as Wilson recovered, Barnett found himself in the reserves. It was to be his regular berth.

TUESDAY 1 OCTOBER 1996

Arsène Wenger officially joined Arsenal from the Japanese side Nagoya Grampus 8 to become the club's first foreign manager.

SATURDAY 2 OCTOBER 1909

Arsenal suffered their worst ever defeat in the First Division, being hammered 7-0 by Blackburn Rovers at Ewood Park. In the 20s Arsenal suffered similar reverses at the hands of West Bromwich Albion (away on 14 October 1922), Newcastle United (away on 3 October 1925) and West Ham United (away on 7 March 1927).

SUNDAY 3 OCTOBER 1999

Patrick Vieira sent off at West Ham in a game that Arsenal lost 2-1 for a foul on Paolo di Canio and as he left the pitch he spat at Neil Ruddock. The action resulted in him being fined £45,000 and banned for six matches. Vieira later said, "What I did was unforgivable, mainly because I'm a role model. My brother is a teacher. If one of his pupils spits at another, he can't tell him not to do it. The kids will just turn around and say, 'Your brother does exactly the same.' But the thing that pisses me off is the £45,000 fine. Coming from where I do, I know the value of money. To my family, that is a phenomenal sum."

SATURDAY 4 OCTOBER 1969

Perennial reserve goalie Geoff Barnett made his debut against Coventry City and Arsenal lost 1-0. Barnett had signed from Everton where he had failed to gain a regular first team place and found himself in the same situation at Highbury where first the brilliance of Bob Wilson and then Jimmy Rimmer kept him out of the team for much of his time at the club.

SATURDAY 4 OCTOBER 1997

Arsenal hero Ian Wright scored his last goal at Highbury in a 5-0 win over Barnsley in the Premier League.

SATURDAY 5 OCTOBER 1889

Royal Arsenal played their first FA Cup match, a qualifying round game against Lyndhurst and won 11-0.

MONDAY 5 OCTOBER 1964

Scottish international Frank McLintock signed for Arsenal from Leicester City for £80,000.

TUESDAY 5 OCTOBER 2004

It was announced that the new venue replacing Arsenal Stadium would be known as the Emirates Stadium for at least 15 years after the airline agreed a £100million sponsorship deal with Arsenal. Beginning in 2006-07 the Emirates would also be the shirt sponsors for eight years.

SATURDAY 6 OCTOBER 1973

Liam Brady made his debut as a substitute for Jeff Blockley in the 1-0 home win against Birmingham City.

SATURDAY 7 OCTOBER 1916

Dr Dicky Roose, who replaced George Burdett as Arsenal's keeper, was killed in action aged 38, serving with the 9th Battalion Royal Fusiliers.

THURSDAY 8 OCTOBER 1931

Arsenal played their first match in the Charity Shield against Sheffield Wednesday at Stamford Bridge. Arsenal won 2-1 with goals from Joe Hulme and David Jack.

SUNDAY 9 OCTOBER 1910

Manager Jack Crayston born at Grange-over-Sands, Lancashire. He became assistant manager to Tom Whittaker in June 1947 becoming caretaker manager on Whittaker's death.

TUESDAY 9 OCTOBER 2001

Former captain Frank McLintock announced he would auction his collection of football memorabilia. He said, "I haven't seen my medals for years. My house was burgled some years ago but fortunately the medals were missed, and since then they have been locked in a bank. There are five gold medals in the collection and the insurance on them to keep them at home is expensive. My shirts and caps are also in storage. I sometimes forget I've got them because I don't see them. I am not struggling for money but I think it is time to cash in and put the proceeds to good use."

TUESDAY 10 OCTOBER 1950

Two Highbury heroes born sixteen years apart. Charlie George and Tony Adams both had problems off the field – George was fined £440 in 1978 for assaulting Jack Spencer, a journalist with *The Eastern Daily Press*. George later commented, "It was the stupidest thing I ever did, but it was totally out of character. I sometimes wonder if I'm remembered more for that than my goal for Arsenal in the cup final." Adams's indiscretions are well-known and appear on other pages in this book.

WEDNESDAY 11 OCTOBER 1972

Jeff Blockley won his solitary England cap in a 1-1 draw against Yugoslavia at Wembley.

SATURDAY 12 OCTOBER 1935

Player-club captain-coach-manager Don Howe born at Springfield, Wolverhampton. He signed for Arsenal in 1964 but retired after breaking his leg in 1966.

SATURDAY 12 OCTOBER 1996

Arsène Wenger took charge of an Arsenal team for the first time as they beat Blackburn Rovers 2-0.

SATURDAY 13 OCTOBER 1928

David Jack became the first player to be sold for a five-figure sum when he joined Arsenal from Bolton Wanderers. Gunners manager Herbert Chapman arranged for the negotiations to held in the bar of the Euston Hotel in London. Bolton wanted £13,000 for the forward. Bob Wall, Chapman's assistant and later general manager and a club director, recalled, "We arrived at the hotel half-an-hour early. Chapman immediately went into the lounge bar. He called the waiter, placed two pound notes in his hand and said, 'George, this is Mr Wall, my assistant. He will drink whisky and dry ginger. I will drink gin and tonic. We shall be joined by guests. They will drink whatever they like. See that our guests are given double of everything, but Mr Wall's whisky and dry ginger will contain no whisky, and my gin and tonic will contain no gin.'" The cunning Chapman persuaded the Bolton contingent to accept £10,890.

SATURDAY 14 OCTOBER 1893

Arsenal achieved their biggest win in the FA Cup in their very first match in the competition beating Ashford United 12-0 at Manor Ground, Plumstead in the first qualifying round. The goals came from Arthur Elliott 3, Jim Henderson 3, Charlie Booth 2, Joe Heath 2, Gavin Crawford and Joe Powell.

TUESDAY 14 OCTOBER 1997

Full-back Jason Crowe made his debut as a 90th minute substitute for Lee Dixon in the third round of the League Cup but was sent off by referee Uriah Rennie 33 seconds later – the fastest debut sending-off in English football history. Jehad Muntasser, a Libyan-born midfielder, came off the subs bench in the 129th minute to replace Luis Boa Morte – 60 seconds later, the referee blew his whistle on the game and on Muntasser's first team career at Arsenal.

SATURDAY 15 OCTOBER 1932

Having started out as a left-half George Male made his first appearance for Arsenal as a right back (in a 3-2 home win over Blackburn Rovers). Unsure of his switch in roles, Male was called into the office of Herbert Chapman and when he left, "I wasn't only convinced I was a right back, I knew I was the best right back in the country".

SATURDAY 16 OCTOBER 2004

Arsenal beat Aston Villa 3-1 to extend their unbeaten run to 49 consecutive league games.

TUESDAY 17 OCTOBER 2000

Veteran goalie John Lukic became the then oldest player to appear in the European Champions League when he was between the sticks in a 1-1 draw away to Lazio.

TUESDAY 18 OCTOBER 2005

Striker Thierry Henry overtook Ian Wright's scoring record of 185 league and cup goals when he hit two goals against Sparta Prague in the Champions League. Wright scored 185 goals between September 1991 and July 1998. Top Premier League goalscorer in three of the past four seasons, he reached the club landmark in 303 games.

TUESDAY 19 OCTOBER 1999

Playing European games at Wembley was never a satisfactory experience and when Barcelona came to visit they beat Arsenal 4-2 at "home".

SATURDAY 20 OCTOBER 1928

Striker David Jack – the first player to score in an FA Cup Final at Wembley and the first player to play for two different clubs in Wembley finals – made his debut for Arsenal against Newcastle United at St James' Park when the Gunners won 3-0.

SATURDAY 20 OCTOBER 1934

Arsenal beat Tottenham Hotspur 5-1 – the biggest home win over the Lillywhites. *The Times* reporter said that Arsenal were expected to win and duly beat Spurs and the 5-1 margin was no more than the Gunners deserved. The crowd of 70,544 watched a superlative performance by Arsenal and *The Times* man added that if both teams had taken all their chances Arsenal could have won 12-3.

SATURDAY 20 OCTOBER 1990

Arsenal went to Old Trafford with an unbeaten record and won 1-0. The match is more remembered for the 21 players (David Seaman was the lone dissenter) becoming involved in a brawl after Nigel Winterburn tackled Denis Irwin. In less than 120 seconds, it was all over but the FA punished both clubs deducting two points from Arsenal and one from United. The Arsenal board were equally unhappy and fined manager George Graham and five players a fortnight's wages.

SATURDAY 21 OCTOBER 1961

Arsenal recorded their biggest ever league win over Manchester United. The Gunners beat the Red Devils 5-1 at Highbury.

SATURDAY 22 OCTOBER 1949

Arsenal's most successful manager Arsène Wenger OBE born at Strasbourg. 6ft 4in Wenger is the only non-British manager to have won the Double in England, and one of the few managers to have done it twice (1998 and 2002). Wenger wasn't always a great success – when he managed Nancy they were relegated but he won the league title in his first season in charge at Monaco.

TUESDAY 22 OCTOBER 1963

Arsenal played their first home match in European competition against Staevnet (Denmark) in the Inter-Cities Fairs Cup. Arsenal lost 3-2 with goals from Alan Skirton and John Barnwell.

MONDAY 22 OCTOBER 2001

Bertie Mee, Arsenal's most successful manager until Arsène Wenger, died at London aged 82 – ironically, on Wenger's birthday.

TUESDAY 23 OCTOBER 2007

Goalie Jens Lehmann, angered at being left out of the side in favour of Manuel Almunia, told German TV station Premiere, "I think – and this is aimed at my dear manager – one shouldn't humiliate players for too long. It's possible that some day I'll feel like talking about the whole issue. At the moment I'm just swallowing it all as part of the humiliation. That's something one has to take in. But I'm an Arsenal player and I won't just fade away quietly. I'm convinced that I'll be playing again. Almunia has not yet showed that he can win matches for us. I've experienced this situation before and know what the others are expecting from the goalkeeper. I can't imagine he'll be able to handle that."

TUESDAY 23 OCTOBER 2007

Arsenal achieved their biggest ever winning margin in the European Champions League beating Slavia Prague 7-0 at the Emirates with Emmanuel Eboué and Theo Walcott bagging a brace each.

WEDNESDAY 24 OCTOBER 1883

Future Arsenal boss George Allison was born at Hurworth-on-Tees, County Durham. Appointed following the death of Herbert Chapman, Allison was content to let his backroom staff runs things on the pitch while he took care of administration and handling the media. Bernard Joy, himself to become a journalist, commented, "[He was] tactful, friendly and good-hearted. But he fell short in his handling of footballers and lacked the professional's deep knowledge of the game."

SATURDAY 24 OCTOBER 1936

The East Stand at Highbury opened albeit over budget at a cost of £130,000. Arsenal didn't really celebrate managing only a 0-0 draw with Grimsby Town.

WEDNESDAY 24 OCTOBER 1956

Manager Tom Whittaker died aged 58 of a heart attack at the University College Hospital, London.

SUNDAY 24 OCTOBER 2004

Pizzagate – Arsenal lost their unbeaten 49-match run to Manchester United 2-0. In the tunnel afterwards the antics continued and someone hit Alex Ferguson with a slice of pizza. Arsène Wenger said that referee Mike Riley had a habit of favouring United and that Van Nistelrooy had cheated. The FA charged Wenger with misconduct and fined him £15,000.

TUESDAY 24 OCTOBER 2006

Left back Armand Traoré made his first team debut in the third round of the Carling Cup against West Bromwich Albion. He was a 24th minute substitute for Emmanuel Adebayor.

SATURDAY 25 OCTOBER 1924

Former Welsh miner Jimmy Brain made his First Division debut against Tottenham Hotspur at Highbury; he scored and Arsenal won 1–0. Well, I say "scored" by Brain. In fact, the ball cannoned into the net off Brain's head from a Jock Rutherford shot that left him unconscious. In September 1931 after more than 200 first-team

appearances and 125 goals, Brain signed for Spurs where he stayed
for four years, including two as player-coach. He realised his folly and
when he retired he returned home to become an Arsenal scout.

SATURDAY 25 OCTOBER 1969

Left-back Sammy Nelson made his first-team debut in the goalless
draw against Ipswich Town at Highbury.

SATURDAY 26 OCTOBER 1889

Royal Arsenal drew 2-2 with Thorpe in the second qualifying round
of the FA Cup but the Gunners went through because Thorpe (later
to become Norwich City) could not afford the fare to London for
the replay.

WEDNESDAY 26 OCTOBER 2005

Former manager and goalie George Swindin died at Kettering
aged 90.

THURSDAY 26 OCTOBER 2006

The Duke of Edinburgh officially opened the Emirates Stadium.
The Queen had also been due to attend but was hampered by a
bad back.

WEDNESDAY 27 OCTOBER 2004

Goalkeeper Manuel Almunia and centre half Philippe Senderos
made their debuts for Arsenal in the 2-1 League Cup victory against
Manchester City at the City of Manchester Stadium.

WEDNESDAY 28 OCTOBER 1998

Remi Garde became the first foreigner to captain Arsenal when he
led the Gunners to a 2-1 victory over Derby County in the third
round of the League Cup at Pride Park Stadium.

TUESDAY 28 OCTOBER 2003

Arsenal beat Rotherham United 9-8 on penalties in the League Cup
in the match that midfielder Cesc Fàbregas made his debut and thus
became Arsenal's youngest player – aged just 16 years and 177 days.
The game ended 1-1 before penalties.

SATURDAY 29 OCTOBER 1983

Centre forward Tony Woodcock became one of the few players to hit five goals in a league match when he hit five at Villa Park as Arsenal thrashed Aston Villa 6-2.

SATURDAY 30 OCTOBER 1937

Central defender Herbie Roberts broke his leg in a 2-1 defeat at home to Middlesbrough. The injury ended his career. That season Arsenal won the First Division title for a fifth time but Roberts missed out on a championship medal because he had played 13 games, one short of the number needed for recognition.

MONDAY 31 OCTOBER 1932

Cliff "Boy" Bastin hit four as Arsenal beat Racing Club de Paris 5-2 in a friendly.

ARSENAL
On This Day

NOVEMBER

FRIDAY 1 NOVEMBER 1996

Midfielder David Hillier moved to Portsmouth for £250,000. Looking at one stage to have a promising career at Highbury, in March 1995, during a drugs test at the Arsenal training ground Hillier tested positive for cannabis but said he had accidentally smoked a spiked cigarette at a party. In January 1996, Hillier appeared in court accused of stealing luggage worth £3,000 at Gatwick Airport. He was fined £750. When Arsène Wenger became manager, Hillier's days at the club were numbered. Now retired, Hillier works as a fireman in Bristol.

WEDNESDAY 1 NOVEMBER 2000

Winger George Armstrong died at Hemel Hempstead Hospital after collapsing with a brain haemorrhage during a session at Arsenal's training ground. Before becoming Arsenal's reserve team coach, he was manager of the Kuwaiti national side until just before Saddam Hussein's invasion. George Graham said, "He was such a thorough professional and a great help to me at Arsenal. As soon as I knew he was available when he was out in the Middle East I jumped at the chance to bring him back." For Arsenal Armstrong made 621 first-team appearances in a 15-year playing career.

SATURDAY 2 NOVEMBER 1907

Woolwich Arsenal met Chelsea in the first all-London match in the First Division and the Blues won 2-1.

WEDNESDAY 2 NOVEMBER 1977

In his second year in charge Arsenal manager Terry Neill splashed out £220,000 to bring Wolverhampton Wanderers striker Alan Sunderland to Highbury.

WEDNESDAY 3 NOVEMBER 1993

Arsenal achieved their biggest ever winning margin in the European Cup Winners' Cup beating Standard Liege 7-0 away in the second leg of the second round having already won 3-0 at Highbury.

SATURDAY 4 NOVEMBER 1972

George Graham made his last Arsenal appearance; the Gunners lost 2-0 at home to Coventry City. Graham left Arsenal for Manchester United.

SUNDAY 4 NOVEMBER 2001

Goalkeeper Richard Wright, 23, managed to punch the ball into his own net during a 4-2 defeat by Charlton Athletic at Highbury.

SATURDAY 5 NOVEMBER 1932

Gillespie Road tube station renamed Arsenal – the only station on the network named after a football club. It was thanks to the lobbying of Herbert Chapman that the London Electric Railway agreed to the change. Arsenal celebrated the change with a resounding 7-1 win over Wolverhampton Wanderers at Molineux.

SATURDAY 5 NOVEMBER 1983

Tony Adams made his first team debut at Highbury in a 2-1 defeat by Sunderland, four weeks after his 17th birthday.

WEDNESDAY 6 NOVEMBER 1968

Left back Bob McNab played against Romania in the first of his four international appearances.

FRIDAY 7 NOVEMBER 2003

Marcus Artry, a promising youth team player who had been with the club for eight years and had represented England at Under-18 level, sent to prison for nine years for his part in three vicious group sex attacks on women and girls as young as 14. The attacks by the gang of four – Artry, 18-year-old Kyle Reid and a 17-year-old and 14-year-old, who both cannot be named for legal reasons – took place between March 2002 and 8 February 2003. Artry was convicted of one charge of rape, one of indecent assault and one of indecency with a child. Sentencing Artry and the 14-year-old, Judge Colin Smith QC said, "I sentence both of you for horrific and terrifying rapes. You both pose a risk of causing serious sexual harm to young women. Women must be protected from you."

WEDNESDAY 8 NOVEMBER 2006

Goalie Mart Poom made his debut for Arsenal as captain in the 1-0 League Cup win against Everton at Goodison Park. He came on as a half-time substitute and took the captain's armband.

SATURDAY 8 NOVEMBER 2008

French midfielder Samir Nasri scored both Gunners goals as Arsenal beat Manchester United 2-1 at the Emirates in a match that saw goalie Manuel Almunia leave the pitch injured, which contributed to the referee Howard Webb adding six minutes of stoppage time.

MONDAY 9 NOVEMBER 1925

Scottish international goalie Bill Harper joined Arsenal from Hibernian with the Gunners paying what was then the record fee of £4,500 for a goalkeeper. He stayed at the club for 19 months before joining Fall River Marksmen in Massachusetts, America. Three years later, after playing for various American teams he returned to Arsenal.

SATURDAY 10 NOVEMBER 1951

Doug Lishman hit a hat-trick as Arsenal beat West Bromwich Albion 6-3 at Highbury.

TUESDAY 11 NOVEMBER 1958

Full-back John Devine born at Dublin, Republic of Ireland and joined Arsenal in November 1974 as an apprentice. He turned professional in 1976.

WEDNESDAY 11 NOVEMBER 1998

Chelsea came to Highbury and inflicted a 5-0 defeat – the heaviest in the League Cup – on the reserve side that Arsène Wenger chose to represent the first team.

SATURDAY 11 NOVEMBER 2000

Goalie John Lukic became Arsenal's oldest player in the Premier League when he played against Derby County at the age of 39 years and 336 days.

SATURDAY 12 NOVEMBER 1932

Arsenal beat Chelsea 1-0 in the first match at which the magnificent West Stand was used – although it would not be opened officially for another month.

SATURDAY 13 NOVEMBER 2004

The highest scoring north London derby: Tottenham Hotspur 4 Arsenal 5. On 37 minutes defender Noureddine Naybet put Spurs ahead. Eight minutes later, Thierry Henry equalised for Arsenal. On 55 minutes, Lauren converted a penalty after Noe Paramot fouled Freddie Ljungberg. After an hour Patrick Vieira made it 3-1 to the Arsenal and the game seemed over. Jermain Defoe scored to make it 3-2 and the game was once more open. Cesc Fàbregas in his first north London derby combined with Henry to give Ljungberg the chance to make it 4-2. Ledley King made it 4-3 before Robert Pirès made it 5-3 and victory for Arsenal. Then Arsenal relaxed and Frederic Kanoute pulled one back for Spurs with two minutes to go. Nine goals, nine different scorers – three points to Arsenal.

WEDNESDAY 14 NOVEMBER 1934

The Battle of Highbury took place between England and Italy – it was Eddie Hapgood's first match as captain of an England side that contained seven Arsenal players. George Allison, the secretary-manager of Arsenal, provided radio commentary and Arsenal trainer Tom Whittaker doubled up as the England man with the magic sponge. Arsenal's George Male and Eddie Hapgood were making their international debuts that day. By half-time England were three to the good. The second half began and, with 58 minutes gone, Italy's brilliant centre-forward Giuseppe "Peppino" Meazza pulled one back. Buoyed by the goal, Italy pushed forward and began playing some skilful football. The brilliance of Frank Moss, in his last international appearance, kept England ahead although he could do nothing on the 62nd minute when Meazza scored to make the score 3-2. That was the way it finished. Eddie Hapgood was later to comment in his autobiography, "It's a bit hard to play when somebody resembling an enthusiastic member of the mafia is scraping his studs down your leg."

SATURDAY 15 NOVEMBER 1952

Arsenal recorded their biggest-ever league victory at Anfield – 5-1 – on their way to winning the First Division title. Ben Marden scored twice and Cliff Holton hit a hat-trick.

FRIDAY 16 NOVEMBER 1962

Former defence stalwart Steve Bould born in Stoke-on-Trent. After retiring he became one of Arsène Wenger's backroom boys looking after the youth squad. Follicly challenged, he once commented, "I think I lost my barnet flicking the ball on for all them years at the near post from Brian Marwood's corners."

MONDAY 17 NOVEMBER 1980

After 829 games for Arsenal at all levels Pat Rice sold to Watford for a bargain basement £8,000. He returned to Arsenal and worked with the youth team and then became caretaker manager while the club waited for Arsène Wenger to arrive.

FRIDAY 18 NOVEMBER 1960

George Eastham joined Arsenal from Newcastle United for £47,500 in a transfer deal that shocked football. He had become increasingly unhappy on Tyneside, claiming that the house the club provided was not fit for human habitation and demanded a transfer. When the club refused to let him go, he went on strike. He complained, "Our contract could bind us to a club for life. It was often the case that the guy on the terrace not only earned more than us — though there's nothing wrong with that — he had more freedom of movement than us." Finally, Newcastle relented but in 1963 Eastham sued them claiming unfair restraint of trade, and that Newcastle owed him £400 in unpaid wages and £650 in unpaid bonuses. Mr Justice Wilberforce ruled partially in Eastham's favour changing forever the way that clubs hired footballers.

SATURDAY 19 NOVEMBER 1887

The beginning of a great footballing rivalry – the first match between Arsenal and Spurs ended a quarter of an hour early because of poor light with Spurs leading 2-1. The reporter for *The Weekly Herald* commended the excellent goalkeeping of Fred Beardsley without whom "the score would have been much larger".

WEDNESDAY 20 NOVEMBER 1968

On the way to Wembley for their first League Cup Final, John Radford scored the only goal of the League Cup semi-final first leg.

WEDNESDAY 21 NOVEMBER 1945

Arsenal plus six "guest players" including Stanley Matthews, Stan Mortensen and Joe Bacuzzi met Moscow Dynamo when the Soviet side toured after the Second World War. The game at Highbury was played in a thick fog and most of the 54,620 fans who turned up saw very little of the match but then nor did the Soviet referee and his two linesmen. Arsenal led 3-2 at half time and rumours reached George Allison that the Soviet man in black would abandon the game if the fog worsened but play on however bad the conditions if it looked like the Muscovites would win. In the end Moscow Dynamo won 4-3.

SATURDAY 21 NOVEMBER 1992

Alan Miller became the first ever Gunners goalkeeper to come on as a substitute as Arsenal lost 3-0 to Leeds United. He also happened to be on the losing side in his last appearance in an Arsenal shirt.

WEDNESDAY 21 NOVEMBER 2001

Unlucky goalkeeper Richard Wright having punched the ball into his own next two months earlier managed to injure himself in a Champions League match against Deportivo La Coruna. To add insult to injury, Arsenal lost 2-1.

WEDNESDAY 21 NOVEMBER 2007

The International Astronomical Union revealed that asteroid 33179 had been renamed Arsène Wenger. His citation read, "Asteroid 33179 Arsenewenger is named to honour the achievements of Arsène Wenger OBE (1949-), a French football manager, who has been manager of Arsenal FC in England since 1996. He is the club's most successful manager in terms of trophies won. In 2004, he became the only manager in Premier League history to go through an entire season undefeated. Wenger's teams are renowned for their beautiful approach to the game. The asteroid, which is between 1.8 and 5.5 miles in diameter, orbits between Mars and Jupiter taking 4.23 years to complete one circuit of the sun."

FRIDAY 21 NOVEMBER 2008

William Gallas sacked as Arsenal captain and dropped from the first team squad after criticising his teammates. The next day Arsenal lost

3-0 to Manchester City at the City of Manchester Stadium with Manuel Almunia donning the captain's armband.

SATURDAY 22 NOVEMBER 1986

Paul Merson made his debut as Arsenal beat Manchester City 3-0 at Highbury.

SATURDAY 22 NOVEMBER 2003

Arsenal beat Birmingham City 3-0 at St Andrew's to go thirteen matches unbeaten from the start of the season breaking the record held by Liverpool. No one could know that Arsenal would go the whole season undefeated.

WEDNESDAY 23 NOVEMBER 1994

Ian Wright scored Arsenal's only goal against Leicester City in the Premier League. The strike ended a run of scoring that had begun 12 games earlier in the European Cup Winners' Cup against Omonia Nicosia (see 15 September 1994).

SUNDAY 24 NOVEMBER 1996

Almost two months after Arsène Wenger took over as manager, Arsenal faced Spurs in the first north London derby of the season. Ian Wright put Arsenal ahead with a penalty after Dennis Bergkamp was fouled. Patrick Vieira went down injured and goalie John Lukic threw the ball out so his teammate could get medical attention. Spurs did not keep to the unwritten agreement to return the ball after an injury and scored virtually from the throw-in helped by an unfortunate bounce that saw Lukic score an own goal. As the game neared its end and the rain beat down on Highbury it looked as if the teams would share the points. With ten minutes to go, John Hartson came on to replace David Platt and seemed to energise the Arsenal side. In the 88th minute, Tony Adams volleyed a left footed shot into the Spurs net. A minute or so later, Bergkamp made it 3-1, slotting past Ian Walker in the Spurs goal.

MONDAY 24 NOVEMBER 2008

Cesc Fàbregas appointed Arsenal captain following the sacking of William Gallas.

SUNDAY 25 NOVEMBER 1984

Pat Jennings made his last Arsenal appearance as the Gunners lost 2-1 to Sheffield Wednesday. In both his first and last games for the club he was on the losing side.

FRIDAY 25 NOVEMBER 1994

Paul Merson confessed to being an alcoholic and cocaine addict. The FA sorted a three-month rehab programme for Merson and he returned to the Arsenal side as a substitute in a nil-nil draw against AC Milan on 1 February 1995, just before George Graham was sacked. Arsenal continued to pay his £5,000-a-week wages while he was in rehab. He said, "I've stayed away from drink and drugs but gambling has beat me, spanked me all over the place. This is one of the biggest killers in the world. Every day it would go through my head about committing suicide."

WEDNESDAY 25 NOVEMBER 1998

Playing their European "home" games at Wembley, 73,707 – the biggest attendance – turned up to watch Arsenal lose 1-0 to RC Lens.

TUESDAY 25 NOVEMBER 2003

Arsenal went to the San Siro and in rain that bucketed down for the entire 90 minutes beat Inter Milan 5-1 in the European Champions League. Thierry Henry hit two, and Freddie Ljungberg, Edu and Robert Pirès completed the rout.

WEDNESDAY 26 NOVEMBER 1958

Winger Danny Clapton became another of Arsenal's one-hit wonder internationals when he made his only appearance for England in a match against Wales at Villa Park which England drew 2-2.

SATURDAY 26 NOVEMBER 1960

David Herd scored all of Arsenal's goals as the Gunners beat Everton 3-2 at Highbury.

SUNDAY 27 NOVEMBER 1938

Arsenal's first team flew on two planes to Paris to play Racing Club in a traditional fixture. The aircraft took off from Croydon but when they came in to land at Le Bourget thick fog had enveloped the French capital. The first plane landed safely but as the second came in to land the pilot realised he would not be able to so he pushed in the throttle to give the plane some power and it soared back into the air – missing the first aircraft and certain death by only a few feet. Even then, the plane was not out of danger. As it rose, the plane narrowly avoided a hangar before gaining height. He circled and came back in safely. The players jumped into taxis for the game. The result was 1-1.

SATURDAY 28 NOVEMBER 1931

Arsenal took Liverpool to pieces in a first division fixture, winning comprehensively 6-0 at Highbury.

WEDNESDAY 28 NOVEMBER 1934

Arsenal won the FA Charity Shield for the second consecutive year, beating Manchester City 4-0. It was the fourth time Arsenal had won the trophy triumphing previously in 1930, 1931 and 1933.

SUNDAY 29 NOVEMBER 1896

Full back Joe Powell died aged 26 just six days after he fell awkwardly while playing Kettering Town and broke his arm. Powell came down with tetanus and blood poisoning. The arm was amputated but to no avail.

SATURDAY 29 NOVEMBER 1930

Arsenal beat Chelsea 5-1 in a London derby to register their biggest win at Stamford Bridge.

THURSDAY 29 NOVEMBER 1984

Arsenal lost to Walsall in a cup tie for the second time. This time they lost 2-1 in the fourth round of the League Cup. It was their first victory at Highbury in nine attempts. Stewart Robson scored Arsenal's solitary goal before a crowd of 22,406.

THURSDAY 30 NOVEMBER 1944

Future Arsenal captain and England caretaker manager Joe Mercer made his Arsenal debut in a 2-2 draw with Bolton Wanderers at Highbury.

THURSDAY 30 NOVEMBER 1944

George Graham, the man who could have had immortality at Arsenal and yet is remembered for all the wrong reasons, born at Bargeddie, Glasgow. Graham joined Arsenal in 1966 and spent six years at Highbury making more than 220 appearances. He returned as manager in 1986 and spent nine years at the club until he was accused of taking a bung. In October 1998 he was appointed manager of the team from the wrong end of the Seven Sisters Road but he was never really accepted at White Hart Lane. It was said that their fans could not bring themselves to chant his name and shouted, "Man in an overcoat's blue and white army."

ARSENAL
On This Day

DECEMBER

SATURDAY 1 DECEMBER 1934

Perhaps he just didn't like clubs from the Midlands. A year before Ted Drake hit seven against Aston Villa, he smashed four against Wolverhampton Wanderers as Arsenal won 7-0 at Highbury.

THURSDAY 1 DECEMBER 1983

Striker Lee Chapman signed for Sunderland for £100,000 having scored just four goals in 23 league games for Arsenal.

THURSDAY 1 DECEMBER 1983

Tommy Caton joined Arsenal from Manchester City for £500,000 following the Maine Road club's relegation. The centre-half made his debut two days later at home to West Bromwich Albion in a 1-0 defeat. Caton became a mainstay in the defence alongside David O'Leary for two years. Caton lost his place to Tony Adams and Martin Keown and was sold to Oxford United in February 1987. He played 95 times for Arsenal scoring three times.

SATURDAY 2 DECEMBER 1967

Right-back Pat Rice made his first-team debut as a substitute for George Graham in a 1-0 league defeat by Burnley at Turf Moor.

TUESDAY 2 DECEMBER 2003

Midfielder Cesc Fàbregas scored his first Arsenal goal in the home 5-1 win over Wolves in the League Cup to become the youngest scorer in the competition.

SATURDAY 3 DECEMBER 1932

Arsenal beat Portsmouth 3-1 at Fratton Park, the fifth consecutive away match that Arsenal had scored three goals or more. The previous results had been 3-2 (Blackburn Rovers), 3-2 (Liverpool), 7-1 (Wolverhampton Wanderers) and 3-5 (Aston Villa). They would not score three goals away from home in five consecutive matches again until 2008-09.

SATURDAY 4 DECEMBER 1909

The first league match between Woolwich Arsenal and Spurs played in the First Division, and Woolwich Arsenal won 1-0.

FRIDAY 4 DECEMBER 1914

Goalie-turned-manager George Swindin born at Campsall, Yorkshire. He joined Arsenal in 1936 for a fee of £4,000. He stayed with the club until 1954 and then returned in 1958 as manager, a job he held for four years.

WEDNESDAY 4 DECEMBER 1974

Scottish midfielder Alex Cropley joined Arsenal from Hibernian. He struggled to make an impact, largely due to injuries and scored six times in 34 games before leaving for Aston Villa in 1976.

SATURDAY 4 DECEMBER 1976

Alan Ball played his last game for Arsenal – a 5-3 win over Newcastle United where former Tyne idol Malcolm Macdonald scored a hat-trick. Not fitting into new manager Terry Neill's plans, Ball was sold to Southampton for £60,000. The squeaky-voiced, red-headed midfield dynamo had played 217 times for the Gunners and scored 52 goals.

MONDAY 5 DECEMBER 1904

Woolwich Arsenal invited a team made up of footballers from various Parisian clubs to a game at the Manor Ground. A crowd of 3,000 turned up to watch the spectacle which turned into something of a French farce – not helped by the French having to borrow an Arsenal reserve called Hodges to make up their 11. The final score was Woolwich Arsenal 26 Paris XI 1. The *Daily Express* reporter rather cruelly, although no doubt accurately, said, "Any one of our school XIs would easily have given the Paris team of yesterday a beating."

TUESDAY 5 DECEMBER 1967

Right-back Pat Rice made his first start for the senior side in the 2-1 League Cup victory against Burnley (albeit playing in the left-back position).

TUESDAY 6 DECEMBER 1955

Striker Tony Woodcock born in Nottingham. He was Arsenal's top scorer for four consecutive years.

SATURDAY 7 DECEMBER 1940

Former Arsenal centre forward Jack Lambert, who had become the club's reserve team coach, was tragically killed in a car accident at Enfield, Middlesex. He was 38.

SUNDAY 8 DECEMBER 1991

Winger Jimmy Carter made his Arsenal debut coming on as a substitute against Nottingham Forest as the Gunners lost 3-2 at the City Ground. He had joined the club from Liverpool two months earlier for £500,000 but never found his feet at Highbury and left on a free transfer in the summer of 1995, having made only 25 league appearances.

SATURDAY 9 DECEMBER 1922

Northern Irish right-back Alec Mackie made his debut for Arsenal in a 1-0 victory against Birmingham City at St Andrew's. Mackie agreed to join Arsenal but in place of a signing-on fee he asked for a pet monkey.

TUESDAY 9 DECEMBER 1975

Arsenal granted their midfield hardman Peter Storey a testimonial. It was watched by 18,813 fans and top Dutch team Feyenoord provided the opposition. Arsenal won 2-1 with goals from midfielders Alan Ball and Liam Brady. After the game both sets of players and sundry others returned to the Jolly Farmers, a pub owned by Storey in Islington, where they enjoyed a two-day lock-in. Other guests included the porn star Mary Millington and singer Olivia Newton-John.

SATURDAY 10 DECEMBER 1932

The Prince of Wales opened the art deco West Stand at Highbury before a match against Chelsea, which Arsenal won 4-1. Designed by Claude Waterlow Ferrier and William Binnie, it cost £45,000.

SATURDAY 10 DECEMBER 1960

After his controversial transfer from Newcastle United George Eastham made his debut for Arsenal against Bolton Wanderers and scored two goals as Arsenal won 5-1.

SUNDAY 10 DECEMBER 2006

Arsenal met Chelsea at Stamford Bridge in the first match since defender Ashley Cole had deserted the Gunners for the Blues. The game ended 1-1. Some Arsenal fans had had fake Bank of Cashley £20 notes printed to wave at the ex-Gunner. In a typically ridiculous over-reaction, the Metropolitan Police Force announced it would arrest anyone seen with the "money". For his part, Cole said, "I am genuine. It's never been about money. For me it's about respect."

SATURDAY 11 DECEMBER 1886

Dial Square FC played their first game winning 6-0 against Eastern Wanderers on a muddy pitch on the Isle of Dogs in east London.

SATURDAY 12 DECEMBER 1896

Arsenal played a league and a cup match in the same day. They fielded a reserve side for the FA Cup and the first team for the league. The league side suffered their biggest ever defeat – and biggest in Division 2 – losing 8-0 away to Loughborough Town, the team that they achieved their biggest ever winning margin against. Meanwhile, the reserves smashed Leyton 5-0 in the cup.

SATURDAY 13 DECEMBER 1975

Reserve keeper Geoff Barnett played his 49th and last game for the Gunners against Stoke City. The following month he left Highbury for good to join Minnesota Kicks in the North American football league.

SATURDAY 14 DECEMBER 1935

Former gas inspector Ted Drake became an Arsenal legend at Villa Park against Aston Villa. Drake began the game carrying an injury, his knee was heavily strapped and then he fell on the perimeter track and cut his arm. Villa took the initiative for the first 15 minutes but by half time Arsenal were three to the good and Drake had a hat-trick. With 60 minutes on the clock, it was 6-0 and Drake had scored two hat-tricks. When the referee blew the whistle the final score was Aston Villa 1 Arsenal 7 with all seven scored by Drake. That day he had nine shots on target – seven went in, Villa keeper Harry Morton saved one and another hit the post and, according to Drake, bounced over the line but the referee disallowed it.

FRIDAY 16 DECEMBER 1983

After a disappointing run of results Terry Neill was sacked as manager by the board and replaced by his coach Don Howe.

SATURDAY 17 DECEMBER 1955

Arsenal beat Blackpool at Highbury. The Gunners were 4-0 up with very little time to go when someone in the crowd blew a whistle. Thinking it was the referee signalling the end of 90 minutes, Arsenal left-back Dennis Evans who had the ball at the time turned and belted it into his own net. The referee had no option but to award the goal to the opposition.

WEDNESDAY 17 DECEMBER 2008

Lady Bracewell-Smith left the Arsenal board of directors causing speculation as to who would buy her 15.9 per cent stake in the club.

SATURDAY 18 DECEMBER 1971

After leaving Arsenal because no one would promise him the manager's job when Bertie Mee stepped down, Don Howe brought his West Bromwich Albion side to Highbury for their first encounter in London since his departure – but it was a miserable north London return: John Roberts scored twice as the Gunners ran out 2-0 winners.

WEDNESDAY 19 DECEMBER 1990

Following his arrest for drink driving, Arsenal skipper Tony Adams appeared at Southend Crown Court where he was jailed for four months. He served half of his sentence (57 days) at Chelmsford Prison as prisoner LE1561 and was freed on Friday 15 February 1991. The following day, as the first team played Leeds United in an FA Cup replay, Adams turned out for the reserves in a 2-2 draw against Reading. On the outside, Adams continued to drink and often played while suffering a hangover.

SATURDAY 20 DECEMBER 1924

Leeds United visited Highbury and then probably wished they hadn't as Arsenal won 6-1.

FRIDAY 21 DECEMBER 1956

Having been caretaker manager for two months Jack Crayston became full-time manager but his reign was not blessed with trophies and he resigned eighteen months later.

WEDNESDAY 22 DECEMBER 1971

Bertie Mee paid a record-breaking £220,000 to bring squeaky-voiced, red-haired midfield dynamo Alan Ball to Highbury.

FRIDAY 23 DECEMBER 1960

Terry Neill scored on his debut in a 1-1 draw against Sheffield Wednesday. He played 275 times for the Gunners before joining Hull City as player-manager in 1970 for a £40,000 fee.

SATURDAY 23 DECEMBER 1978

One of the great performances by an Arsenal side at White Hart Lane with a hat-trick from Alan Sunderland and a world class game from Liam Brady as the Gunners romped home 5-0. Pat Jennings returned to White Hart Lane for the first time since his move to Highbury in August 1977 but the Spurs forwards did not trouble him.

SATURDAY 24 DECEMBER 1932

Arsenal gave fans an early Christmas present as they beat Sheffield United 9-2 at Highbury. Jack Lambert hit five of the goals while Cliff Bastin scored a hat-trick.

SATURDAY 25 DECEMBER 1886

Fifteen members of Dial Square FC officially adopted the title of Royal Arsenal at a meeting in The Royal Oak pub.

WEDNESDAY 25 DECEMBER 1918

The first manager to lead Arsenal to the Double Bertie Mee born at Bulwell, Nottinghamshire. Mee joined the club in 1960 as a physiotherapist and became manager after Billy Wright was sacked in 1966. He resigned after ten years in the job.

25 DECEMBER

When Woolwich Arsenal moved to Highbury, they had to give an undertaking that they would not play games on Christmas Day or Good Friday. The promise was not broken until they bought the lease in 1925. These are those Christmas Day contests – pre- and post-Highbury.

1894...Woolwich Arsenal 7 Port Vale 0
1895...Woolwich Arsenal 2 Port Vale 1
1896...............................Woolwich Arsenal 6 Lincoln City 2
1901...Woolwich Arsenal 0 Blackpool 0
1903............................... Woolwich Arsenal 4 Bradford City 1
1905.......................... Woolwich Arsenal 4 Newcastle United 3
1907.......................... Woolwich Arsenal 2 Newcastle United 2
1909.......................... Woolwich Arsenal 0 Newcastle United 3
1912........................Woolwich Arsenal 0 Notts County 0
1925...Arsenal 3 Notts County 0
1934................................... Arsenal 5 Preston North End 3
1936................................... Arsenal 4 Preston North End 1
1946...................................... Arsenal 2 Portsmouth 1
1948......................................Arsenal 3 Derby County 3
1950..Arsenal 0 Stoke City 3
1951...................................... Arsenal 4 Portsmouth 1
1954.. Arsenal 1 Chelsea 0

THURSDAY 26 DECEMBER 1929

Club captain Tom Parker played his 172nd consecutive game for the Gunners.

TUESDAY 26 DECEMBER 2000

Thierry Henry hit the first hat-trick of his Arsenal career as the Gunners walloped Leicester City 6-1 at Highbury.

MONDAY 27 DECEMBER 1971

World Cup winning midfielder Alan Ball made his debut for Arsenal against Nottingham Forest in a 1-1 draw at the City Ground in which George Graham scored Arsenal's goal. In 1974 Ball was appointed club captain.

THURSDAY 27 DECEMBER 2007

Nicklas Bendtner scored the fastest goal by a substitute in the Premier League when he hit the back of the net after just six seconds against Spurs.

FRIDAY 28 DECEMBER 2008

Arsenal beat Portsmouth 1-0 – it was the first of what would be eight consecutive home clean sheets for goalie Manuel Almunia. The record ended against Chelsea when Łukasz Fabiański was between the posts.

SATURDAY 29 DECEMBER 1990

Regarded by many as the one that got away, Andy Cole played his only Arsenal league game coming on as sub in a 4-1 home victory over Sheffield United.

SATURDAY 30 DECEMBER 2000

A rare goal from Lee Dixon – he scored 28 in almost 600 appearances – as Arsenal drew 2-2 at home to Sunderland.

SATURDAY 31 DECEMBER 1994

Danish midfielder John Jensen scored his only Arsenal goal as the Gunners lost 3-1 to Queens Park Rangers at Highbury.

BOOKS

Adams, Tony with Ian Ridley
Addicted
(Ted Smart, 1998)

Baily, Philip, Philip Thorn & Peter Wynne-Thomas
Who's Who of Cricketers
(Newnes Books, 1984)

Donnelley, Paul
The Arsenal Companion
(Pitch, 2008)

Fox, Norman
Farewell to Highbury The Arsenal Story
(The Bluecoat Press, 2006)

Frindall, Bill
The Guinness Book Of Cricket Facts And Feats
(Guinness Superlatives, 1983)

Harris, Jeff
Arsenal Who's Who
(Independent UK Sports Publications, 1995)

Hayes, Dean
Arsenal The Football Facts
(John Blake, 2007)

Jennings, Pat in association with Reg Drury
An Autobiography
(Granada, 1984)

Maidment, Jem
Arsenal 100 Greatest Games
(Hamlyn, 2005)

The Official Arsenal Encyclopaedia
(Hamlyn, 2008)

Marinello, Peter with Will Price
Fallen Idle Autobiography
(Headline, 2007)

Matthews, Tony
Who's Who of Arsenal
(Mainstream, 2007)

McLintock, Frank with Rob Bagchi
True Grit The Autobiography
(Headline, 2005)

Neill, Terry
Revelations Of A Football Manager
(Sidgwick & Jackson, 1985)

Newkey-Burden, Chas
Arsenal Premiership Player Profiles
(Hamlyn, 2007)

Ollier, Fred
Arsenal A Complete Record 1886-1988
(Breedon Books, 1988)

Poll, Graham
Seeing Red
(HarperSport, 2008)

Ponting, Ivan
Arsenal Player-by-Player
(Hamlyn, 1996, 2004)

Shaw, Phil
The Book of Football Quotations
(Ebury Press, 2008)

Soar, Phil and Martin Tyler
The Official Illustrated History of Arsenal 1886-2008
(Hamlyn, 2008)

Spurling, Jon
Rebels for the Cause The Alternative History of Arsenal FC
(Mainstream, 2003)

Waring, Peter
Arsenal Head to Head
(Breedon Books, 2004)

Wilson, Bob
Behind The Network My Autobiography
(Coronet Books, 2004)

MAGAZINES

Official Arsenal Magazine
Official Arsenal Match Day programmes

WEBSITES

arsenal-mania.com
en.wikipedia.org
www.anfield-online.co.uk
www.arseweb.com
www.arsenal.com
www.arsenal-land.co.uk
www.arsenal-world.co.uk
www.bbc.co.uk
www.goonernews.com
www.historicalkits.co.uk/Arsenal/Arsenal.htm
www.premierleague.com/page/arsenal
www.soccerbase.com
www.thesun.co.uk
www.timesonline.co.uk
www.Uefa.com
www.ynwa.tv

NEWSPAPERS

*Daily Mirror, Evening Standard,
The Irish Independent, The Sun, The Times.*